Modern Critical Interpretations

George Bernard Shaw's Saint Joan

Modern Critical Interpretations

These and other titles in preparation

Modern Critical Interpretations

George Bernard Shaw's
Saint Joan

Edited and with an introduction by

Harold Bloom
Sterling Professor of the Humanities
Yale University

Chelsea House Publishers ◊ *1987*

NEW YORK ◊ NEW HAVEN ◊ PHILADELPHIA

© 1987 by Chelsea House Publishers,
a division of Chelsea House Educational Communications, Inc.,
  95 Madison Avenue, New York, NY 10016
  345 Whitney Avenue, New Haven, CT 06511
  5014 West Chester Pike, Edgemont, PA 19028

Introduction © 1987 by Harold Bloom

Printed and bound in the United States of America

∞ The paper used in this publication meets the minimum
requirements of the American National Standard for
Permanence of Paper for Printed Library Materials,
Z39.48–1984.

Library of Congress Cataloging-in-Publication Data
George Bernard Shaw's Saint Joan.
  (Modern critical interpretations)
  Bibliography: p.
  Includes index.
  1. Shaw, Bernard, 1856–1950. Saint Joan. 2. Joan,
of Arc, Saint, 1412–1431, in fiction, drama, poetry,
etc. I. Bloom, Harold. II. Series.
PR5363.S33G46 1987   822'.912   86–33453
ISBN 1-55546-030-5 (alk. paper)

Contents

Editor's Note

This book brings together a representative selection of the best criticism that has been devoted to George Bernard Shaw's *Saint Joan*. The critical essays are reprinted here in the chronological order of their original publication. I am grateful to Marena Fisher for her aid in editing this volume.

My introduction first centers upon Shaw's religion, Creative Evolution, and then traces the design of that religion in *Saint Joan*. The chronological sequence of criticism begins with a classic essay by Louis L. Martz that contrasts Shaw's saint as tragic hero to T. S. Eliot's in *Murder in the Cathedral*. Martz urges us to see Eliot's drama as an "affirmative tragedy," while Shaw's is just barely tragic, being after all a tragicomedy, as I would agree.

Louis Crompton reads *Saint Joan* by way of the Hegelian approach to tragedy and also describes Joan's fortunes in literature. Juxtaposing *Saint Joan* to *Caesar and Cleopatra*, Margery M. Morgan explores the contours of Shaw's history plays and finds in Joan a heroine of the exploring impulse. Charles A. Berst, considering *Saint Joan* as poetic drama, gives us a very full reading of the entire play.

Concentrating upon Shaw's beliefs, some of them rather weird, William Searle contrasts Joan to Shaw, mystical saint compared to vitalistic skeptic with a metabiological belief in "sane hallucinations." Nicholas Grene, in this book's final essay, emphasizes that Shaw's religion, "rational irrationalism without mystery," prevented his having a tragic vision of Joan, yet could not keep his imagination from going out to the most surprising of his heroines.

Introduction

"With the single exception of Homer there is no eminent writer, not even Sir Walter Scott, whom I despise so entirely as I despise Shakespear when I measure my mind against his." Shaw, obsessive polemicist, would write anything, even that unfortunate sentence. No critic would wish to measure Shaw's mind against Shakespeare's, particularly since originality was hardly Shaw's strength. Shavian ideas are quarried from Schopenhauer, Nietzsche, Ibsen, Wagner, Ruskin, Samuel Butler, Shelley, Carlyle, Marx (more or less), William Morris, Lamarck, Bergson—the list could be extended. Though an intellectual dramatist, Shaw essentially popularized the concepts and images of others. He continues to hold the stage and might appear to have earned his reputation of being the principal writer of English comic drama since Shakespeare. Yet his limitations are disconcerting, and the experience of rereading even his most famous plays, after many years away from them, is disappointingly mixed. They are much more than period pieces, but they hardly seem to be for all time. No single comedy by Shaw matches Wilde's *The Importance of Being Earnest* or the tragic farces of Beckett.

Eric Bentley best demonstrated that Shaw viewed himself as a prose prophet in direct succession to Carlyle, Ruskin, and Morris. This is the Shaw of the prefaces, of *Essays in Fabian Socialism,* of *Doctors' Delusions, Crude Criminology, Sham Education.* Only the prefaces to the plays are still read, and of course they are not really prefaces to the plays. They expound Shaw's very odd personal religion, the rather cold worship of Creative Evolution. Of this religion, one can say that it is no more bizarre than most, and less distasteful than many, but it is still quite grotesque. To judge religions by aesthetic criteria may seem perverse, but what others are relevant for poems, plays, stories, novels, personal essays? By any aesthetic standard, Shaw's heretical faith is considerably less interesting or impressive than D. H. Lawrence's barbaric vitalism in *The Plumed Serpent* or even Thomas Hardy's negative homage to the Immanent Will in *The Dynasts*.

G. K. Chesterton, in his book on Shaw (1909), observed that the heroine of *Major Barbara*

> ends by suggesting that she will serve God without personal hope, so that she may owe nothing to God and He owe everything to her. It does not seem to strike her that if God owes everything to her He is not God. These things affect me merely as tedious perversions of a phrase. It is as if you said, "I will never have a father unless I have begotten him."

"He who is willing to do the work gives birth to his own father," Kierkegaard wrote, and Nietzsche mused that: "If one hasn't had a good father, then it is necessary to invent one." Shaw was neither a Darwinian nor a Freudian, and I think he was a bad Nietzschean, who had misread rather weakly the sage of *Zarathustra*. But in his life he had suffered an inadequate father, and certainly he was willing to do the work. Like his own Major Barbara, he wished to have a God who would owe everything to G. B. S. That requires a writer to possess superb mythopoeic powers, and fortunately for Shaw his greatest literary strength was as an inventor of new myths. Shaw endures in a high literary sense and remains eminently readable as well as actable because of his mythmaking faculty, a power he shared with Blake and Shelley, Wagner and Ibsen. He was not a stylist, not a thinker, not a psychologist, and utterly lacked even an iota of the uncanny Shakespearean ability to represent character and personality with overwhelming persuasiveness. His dialogue is marred by his garrulous tendencies, and the way he embodied his ideas is too often wearisomely simplistic. Yet his dramas linger in us because his beings transcend their inadequate status as representations of the human, with which he was hopelessly impatient anyway. They suggest something more obsessive than daily life, something that moves and has its being in the cosmos we learn to call Shavian, a comic version of Schopenhauer's terrible world dominated by the remorseless Will to Live.

As a critic, Shaw was genial only where he was not menaced, and he felt deeply menaced by the Aesthetic vision, of which his Socialism never quite got free. Like Oscar Wilde and Wilde's mentor Walter Pater, Shaw was the direct descendant of Ruskin, and his animus against Wilde and Pater reflects the anxiety of an ambitious son toward rival claimants to a heritage. Pater insisted upon style, as did Wilde, and Shaw has no style to speak of, not much more, say, than Eugene O'Neill. Reviewing Wilde's *An Ideal Husband* on January 12, 1895, for Frank Harris's *Saturday Review*, Shaw was both generous and just:

> Mr Wilde, an arch-artist, is so colossally lazy that he trifles even with the work by which an artist escapes work. He distils the very quintessence, and gets as product plays which are so unapproachably playful that they are the delight of every playgoer with twopenn'orth of brains.

A month later, confronted by *The Importance of Being Earnest: A Trivial Comedy for Serious People,* Shaw lost his composure, his generosity, and his sense of critical justice:

> I cannot say that I greatly cared for The Importance of Being Earnest. It amused me, of course; but unless comedy touches me as well as amuses me, it leaves me with a sense of having wasted my evening. I go to the theatre to be moved to laughter, not to be tickled or bustled into it; and that is why, though I laugh as much as anybody at a farcical comedy, I am out of spirits before the end of the second act, and out of temper before the end of the third, my miserable mechanical laughter intensifying these symptoms at every outburst. If the public ever becomes intelligent enough to know when it is really enjoying itself and when it is not, there will be an end of farcical comedy. Now in The Importance of Being Earnest there is plenty of this rib-tickling: for instance, the lies, the deceptions, the cross purposes, the sham mourning, the christening of the two grown-up men, the muffin eating, and so forth. These could only have been raised from the farcical plane by making them occur to characters who had, like Don Quixote, convinced us of their reality and obtained some hold on our sympathy. But that unfortunate moment of Gilbertism breaks our belief in the humanity of the play.

Would it be possible to have a sillier critical reaction to the most delightful comic drama in English since Shakespeare? Twenty-three years later, Shaw wrote a letter (if it is that) to Frank Harris, published by Harris in his *Life of Wilde* (1918), and then reprinted by Shaw in his *Pen Portraits and Reviews*. Again Wilde was an artist of "stupendous laziness," and again he was indicted, this time after his death, for heartlessness:

> Our sixth meeting, the only other one I can remember, was the one at the Café Royal. On that occasion he was not too preoccupied with his danger to be disgusted with me because I, who had praised his first plays handsomely, had turned traitor over The Importance of Being Earnest. Clever as it was, it was his first really heartless play. In the others the chivalry of the eighteenth-century Irishman and the romance of the disciple of Théophile Gautier (Oscar was old-fashioned in the Irish way, except as a critic of morals) not only gave a certain kindness and gallantry to the serious passages and to the handling of the women, but provided that proximity of emotion without which laughter, however irresistible, is destructive and sinister. In The Importance of Being Earnest this had vanished; and the play, though extremely funny, was essentially hateful. I had no idea that Oscar was going to the dogs, and that this represented a real degeneracy produced by his debaucheries. I thought he was still developing; and I hazarded the unhappy guess that The Importance of Being Earnest was in idea a young work written or projected long before under the influence of Gilbert and furbished up for Alexander as a potboiler. At the Café Royal that day I calmly asked him whether I was not right. He indignantly repudiated my guess, and said loftily (the only time he ever tried on me the attitude he took to John Gray and his more abject disciples) that he was disappointed in me. I suppose I said, "Then what on earth has happened to you?" but I recollect nothing more on that subject except that we did not quarrel over it.

Shaw remains unique in finding *The Importance of Being Earnest* (of all plays!) "essentially hateful." A clue to this astonishing reaction can be found in Shaw's outraged response to Max Beerbohm's review of *Man and Superman,* as expressed in his letter to Beerbohm, on September 15, 1903:

> You idiot, do you suppose I dont know my own powers? I tell you in this book as plainly as the thing can be told, that the reason Bunyan reached such a pitch of mastery in literary art (and knew it) whilst poor Pater could never get beyond a nerveless amateur affectation which had not even the common workaday quality of vulgar journalism (and, alas! didnt know it, though he died of his own futility), was that it was life or death with the tinker to make people understand his message and see his vision, whilst Pater had neither message nor vision & only wanted to cultivate style, with the result that of the two attempts I have made to read him the first broke down at the tenth sentence & the second at the first. Pater took a genteel walk up Parnassus: Bunyan fled from the wrath to come: that explains the difference in their pace & in the length they covered.

Poor Pater is dragged in and beaten up because he was the apostle of style, while Bunyan is summoned up supposedly as the model for Shaw, who also has a message and a vision. It is a little difficult to associate *The Pilgrim's Progress* with *Man and Superman,* but one can suspect shrewdly that Pater here is a surrogate for Wilde, who had achieved an absolute comic music of perfect style and stance in *The Importance of Being Earnest.* Shavians become indignant at the comparison, but Shaw does poorly when one reads, side by side, any of the *Fabian Essays* and Wilde's extraordinary essay, "The Soul of Man under Socialism." Something even darker happens when we juxtapose *Man and Superman* with *The Importance of Being Earnest,* but then Shaw is not unique in not being able to survive such a comparison.

II

Saint Joan (1923) is a work written against its own literary age, the era of Proust, Joyce, Kafka, and above all others, Freud. It seems astonishing that *Saint Joan* is contemporary with Eliot's *The Waste Land* (1922). Eliot, whose own once-fashionable neo-Christianity now seems a refined superstition, rejected Shaw with his customary generosity of spirit: "The potent ju-ju of the Life Force is a gross superstition." That might be De Stogumber crying out as he drags Joan out to be burned in Shaw's play, but then Eliot had become more English than the English. Luigi Pirandello, Shaw's peer as dramatist (as Eliot was not; *Murder in the Cathedral* weirdly concludes with a blatant imitation of the end of *Saint Joan*) made the inevitably accurate comment on the play, which is that it could as well have been called *Saint Bernard Shaw*:

> Joan, at bottom, quite without knowing it, and still declaring herself a faithful daughter of the Church, is a Puritan, like Shaw himself—affirming her own life impulse, her unshakable, her even tyrannical will to live, by accepting death itself.

That "tyrannical will to live" is once again Shaw's revision of Schopenhauer by way of Ruskin and Lamarck—the only wealth is life, as Ruskin taught, and the will creatively modifies the evolution of life in the individual, as Shaw strongly misread Lamarck. Eric Bentley, always the brilliantly sympathetic defender of Shaw, reads *Saint Joan* as a triumphant resolution of Shaw's worn-out agon between system and vitality, between society and the individual, a resolution that is comprised of an exactly equal sympathy for the old antagonists. The sympathy cannot be denied, but the play is overwhelmingly Protestant, and its rhetoric wars against its argument and so takes the side of Joan.

What precisely *is* Joan's religion, which is to ask, Can we make a coherent doctrine out of the religion of Bernard Shaw—his religion as a dramatist rather than as G. B. S., the polemicist and public personality? Did he indeed believe that what he called the Evolutionary Appetite was "the only surviving member of the Trinity," the Holy Spirit? Milton, Shaw's greatest precursor as exalter of the Protestant Will and its holy right of private judgment, had invoked that Spirit as one that descended, in preference to all temples, in order to visit the pure and upright heart—of John Milton in particular. We know how prophetically serious Milton was in this declaration, and his sublime rhetoric persuades us to wrestle with his self-election. But what are we to do with Shaw, whose rhetoric perhaps can beguile us sometimes but never can persuade?

Joan, like Shaw, does very well without either God the Father or Jesus Christ His Son. Though her ghost concludes the epilogue by addressing the "God that madest this beautiful earth," she does not intend her auditor to be the Jehovah of Genesis. Her initial divine reference in the play is to "orders from my Lord," but immediately she tells us that "that is the will of God that you are to do what He has put into my mind," which means that her own will simply is the will of God. Since she is, like Shaw, an Anglo-Irish Protestant, she never once invokes Jesus or His Mother. Instead, she listens to the voices of "the blessed saints Catherine and Margaret, who speak to me every day," and who might as well be girls from her own village. Her battle cry is: "Who is for God and His Maid?" And her last words, before she is pushed off stage to the stake, make clear that she is Shaw's substitute for Jesus of Nazareth:

> His ways are not your ways. He wills that I go through the fire to His bosom; for I am His child, and you are not fit that I should live among you. This is my last word to you.

In the queer but effective *The Adventures of the Black Girl in Her Search for God,* Shaw has his surrogate, whose "face was all intelligence," explain to the black girl his doctrine of work: "For we shall never be able to bear His full presence until we have fulfilled all His purposes and become gods ourselves. . . . If our work were done we should be of no further use: that would be the end of us." Carlyle would have winced at our becoming gods ourselves, but the gospel of labor remains essentially Carlyle's and Ruskin's. Defending *The Black Girl* in a letter to a friendly but pugnacious Abbess, Shaw associated himself with the prophet Micah and refused to take as his idea of God "the anti-vegetarian deity who, after trying to exterminate the human race by drowning it, was coaxed out of finishing the job by a gorgeous smell of roast meat." That is good enough fun, but we return to *Saint Joan* to ask a question that has nothing in common with the Anglo-Catholic Eliot's indictment of a gross superstition. Vocabulary aside, is Joan at all interested in God, any God at all? Is Shaw?

If the term "God" is to retain any crucial aspect of its biblical range of reference, then Joan and Shaw could not care less. The Life Force has no personality, whereas Jehovah most certainly does, however uncomfortable it makes us. Is Joan anything except an embodiment of the Life Force? Has Shaw endowed her with a personality? Alas, I think not. The play holds the stage, but that will not always be true. Shaw's rhetoric is not provident or strong enough to give us the representation of a coherent psychology in Joan. The figure of the first few scenes has nothing in common with the heroine who repudiates her own surrender at the trial or with the shade of a saint who appears to the King of France in his dream that forms the epilogue. No development or unfolding authentically links the country girl with the martyr.

Shaw's bravura as a dramatist saves the play as a performance piece but cannot make it into enduring literature. Its humor works; its caricatures amuse us; its ironies, though too palpable, provoke analysis and argument. But Joan, though she listens to voices, cannot change by listening to her own voice speaking, which is what even the minor figures in Shakespeare never fail to do. Creative Evolution, as a literary religion, could not do for Shaw what he could not do for himself. In *Saint Joan,* he fails at representing persons, since they are more than their ideas.

The Saint as Tragic Hero: *Saint Joan* and *Murder in the Cathedral*

Louis L. Martz

Can a saint's play ever be truly tragic? This is the problem we must explore today, for saints and martyrs have frequently been regarded as impossible subjects for true tragedy. The reasons have been forcibly summed up by Butcher in his standard commentary on Aristotle's *Poetics*. One trouble is, he says, that Goodness "is apt to be immobile and uncombative. In refusing to strike back it brings the action to a standstill." This is exactly the objection sometimes made to Eliot's presentation of Becket, who is certainly immobile and, in a sense, uncombative:

> We are not here to triumph by fighting, by stratagem, or
> > by resistance,
> Not to fight with beasts as men. We have fought the
> > beast
> And have conquered. We have only to conquer
> Now, by suffering.

But even in the case of more combative saints, such as Joan of Arc, [S. H.] Butcher would see a serious difficulty: "Impersonal ardour in the cause of right," he says, does not have "the same dramatic fascination as the spectacle of human weakness or passion doing battle with the fate it has brought upon itself." And in short, the chief

From *Tragic Themes in Western Literature,* edited by Cleanth Brooks. © 1955 by Yale University Press.

difficulty is that "the death of the martyr presents to us not the defeat, but the victory of the individual; the issue of a conflict in which the individual is ranged on the same side as the higher powers, and the sense of suffering consequently lost in that of moral triumph." This, I suppose, is what I. A. Richards also means when he declares [in *Principles of Literary Criticism*] that "The least touch of any theology which has a compensating Heaven to offer the tragic hero is fatal"—fatal, that is, to the tragic effect. But we remember:

> Good night, sweet prince,
> And flights of angels sing thee to thy rest.

And we remember the transfiguration of Oedipus at Colonus. Hamlet and Oedipus, we might argue, are in the end on the side of the higher powers. I do not know what we should call Oedipus at Colonus, if he is not a kind of saint, and there is something almost saintly in Hamlet's acute sensitivity to evil. Butcher concedes that Aristotle does not take account of this exceptional type of tragedy "which exhibits the antagonism between a pure will and a disjointed world." We are drawn, then, into some discussion of the nature of tragedy, into some discussion of the plight of tragedy today, and into some discussion, also, of another excellent kind of writing, sometimes called tragic, in which the modern world has achieved a peculiar eminence.

Let us begin with this other kind, for it is a kind without a touch of any theology. I am thinking of the kind represented by the recent admirable movie, *A Place in the Sun,* or by Hemingway's *A Farewell to Arms.* I am thinking particularly of the attitude represented by dying words of Hemingway's heroine: " 'I'm going to die,' she said; then waited and said, 'I hate it' . . . Then a little later, 'I'm not afraid. I just hate it.' . . . 'Don't worry, darling, . . . I'm not a bit afraid. It's just a dirty trick.' " This scene is painful and pitiful as all that earlier misery in the same novel, during the rainy retreat from Caporetto, at the beginning of which Hemingway's hero sums up the central impact of the book, in words that are often quoted: "I was always embarrassed by the words sacred, glorious, and sacrifice and the expression in vain." And he proceeds to emphasize his embarrassment in words that echo a biblical cadence, faintly, and ironically: "We had heard them, sometimes standing in the rain almost out of earshot, so that only the shouted words came through, and had read them, on proclamations that were slapped up by billposters over other proclamations, now for a long time, and I had seen nothing sacred, and the things that were glorious had no glory and the sacrifices were like the stockyards at Chicago if nothing was done with the meat except to bury it."

The tragedies of Oedipus, Phèdre, Samson, or Hamlet certainly include something like this sense of shattered illusions, this painful recognition of man's fragility, and this pitiful recognition of the inadequacy of human love—but along with, in the same moment with, equally powerful affirmations of the validity of these terms sacred, glorious, sacrifice, and the expression in vain. Tragedy seems simultaneously to doubt and to believe in such expressions: tragedy seems never to know what Wallace Stevens calls "an affirmation free from doubt"—and yet it always seems to contain at least the ghost of an affirmation. Oedipus the King and Samson Agonistes, blind and erring, still sacrifice themselves "gloriously," as Milton puts it. Racine's drama of Phèdre affirms the validity of the law of reason, even as the heroine dissolves herself in passion. And Hamlet sees mankind, simultaneously, as the most angelical and the most vicious of earthly creatures; like the chorus of *Murder in the Cathedral,* Hamlet "knows and does not know."

This sense of a double vision at work in tragedy is somewhat akin to I. A. Richards's famous variation on Aristotle, where Richards finds the essence of tragedy to reside in a "balanced poise." In the "full tragic experience," Richards declares, "there is no suppression. The mind does not shy away from anything." But Richards himself, like Hemingway's hero, then proceeds to shy away from transcendental matters, when he declares that the mind, in tragedy, "stands uncomforted, unintimidated, alone and self-reliant." This, it seems, will not quite square with Richards's ultimate account of tragedy as "perhaps the most general, all-accepting, all-ordering experience known."

A clearer account, at least a more dogmatic account, of this double vision of tragedy has been set forth by Joyce in his *Portrait of the Artist.* "Aristotle has not defined pity and terror," says Stephen Dedalus, "I have." "Pity is the feeling which arrests the mind in the presence of whatsoever is grave and constant in human sufferings and unites it with the human sufferer. Terror is the feeling which arrests the mind in the presence of whatsoever is grave and constant in human sufferings and unites it with the secret cause." Tragedy, then, seems to demand both the human sufferer and the secret cause:

that is to say, the doubt, the pain, the pity of the human sufferer; and the affirmation, the awe, the terror of the secret cause. It is an affirmation even though the cause is destructive in its immediate effects: for this cause seems to affirm the existence of some universal order of things.

From this standpoint we can estimate the enormous problem that faces the modern writer in his quest for tragedy. For with Ibsen, as we have seen, this power of double vision is in some difficulty. In *Ghosts* or in *Rosmersholm* the element of affirmation is almost overwhelmed by the horror and the suffering that come from the operation of the secret cause—here represented by the family heritage —the dead husband, the dead wife. The affirmation is present, however, as Mr. Reichardt has pointed out, in the salvation of an individual's integrity. Ibsen's *Ghosts,* which has the rain pouring down outside for most of the play, nevertheless ends with a view of bright sunshine on the glaciers: symbolizing, perhaps, the clear self-realization which the heroine has achieved. But it is not a very long step before we exit—left—from these shattered drawing rooms into the rain of Ernest Hemingway, where we have the human sufferers, "alone and self-reliant," without a touch of any secret cause. We are in the world of pity which Santayana has beautifully described in a passage of his *Realms of Being,* where he speaks of the "unreasoning sentiment" he might feel in seeing a "blind old beggar" in a Spanish town: "pity simply, the pity of existence, suffusing, arresting, rendering visionary the spectacle of the moment and spreading blindly outwards, like a light in the dark, towards objects which it does not avail to render distinguishable."

It seems a perfect account of the central and powerful effect achieved in many of the best efforts of the modern stage, or movie, or novel, works of pity, where pity dissolves the scene, resolves it into the dew that Hamlet considers but transcends. Thus *A Farewell to Arms* is enveloped in symbolic rain; in *The Naked and the Dead* humanity is lost in the dim Pacific jungle; and the haze of madness gradually dissolves the realistic setting of *A Streetcar Named Desire* or *Death of a Salesman.* In the end, Willy Loman has to plant his garden in the dark. "The pity of existence . . . spreading blindly outwards . . . towards objects which it does not avail to render distinguishable."

The problem of the tragic writer in our day appears to be: how to control this threatened dissolution, how to combine this "unreasoning sentiment" with something like the different vision that Santayana goes on to suggest: "Suppose now that I turn through the town gates and suddenly see a broad valley spread out before me with the purple sierra in the distance beyond. This expanse, this vastness, fills my intuition; also, perhaps, some sense of the deeper breath which I draw as if my breast expanded in sympathy with the rounded heavens." Thus we often find that the modern writer who seeks a tragic effect will attempt, by some device, such as Ibsen's family heritage or his view of the glacier, to give us the experience of a secret cause underlying his work of pity—to give it broader dimensions, sharper form, to render the ultimate objects distinguishable, to prevent it from spreading blindly outwards. We can see this plainly in O'Neill's *Mourning Becomes Electra,* where O'Neill, by borrowing from Aeschylus the ancient idea of a family curse, is able to give his drama a firm, stark outline and to endow his heroine with something like a tragic dignity. The only trouble is that this Freudian version of a family curse is not secret enough: it tends to announce itself hysterically, all over the place: "I'm the last Mannon. I've got to punish myself!" In the end we feel that this family curse has been shipped in from Greece and has never quite settled down in New England.

Eliot has described much the same difficulty which appears in his play *The Family Reunion,* where he too, even more boldly than O'Neill, has tried to borrow the Furies from Aeschylus. Eliot deploys his Furies, quite impolitely, in the middle of Ibsen's drawing room. As we might expect, they were not welcome: "We tried every possible manner of presenting them," says Eliot. "We put them on the stage, and they looked like uninvited guests who had strayed in from a fancy-dress ball. We concealed them behind gauze, and they suggested a still out of a Walt Disney film. We made them dimmer, and they looked like shrubbery just outside the window. I have seen other expedients tried": Eliot adds, "I have seen them signalling from across the garden, or swarming onto the stage like a football team, and they are never right. They never succeed in being either Greek goddesses or modern spooks. But their failure," he concludes, "is merely a symptom of the failure to adjust the ancient with the modern." Or, we might say, a failure to adjust the ancient Aeschylean symbol of a secret cause with the modern human sufferer.

How, then, can it be done? It is in their approach to this problem that *Saint Joan* and *Murder in the Cathedral* reveal their peculiar power, an approach that seems to have been made possible by this fact: that both Shaw and Eliot feel they cannot depend upon their audience to accept their saintly heroes as divinely inspired. The dramaturgy of both plays is based upon a deliberate manipulation of the elements of religious skepticism or uncertainty in the audience.

As Eliot's play moves toward the somber conclusion of its first half, the Four Tempters cry out in the temptation of self-pity ("It's just a dirty trick"):

> Man's life is a cheat and a disappointment . . .
> All things become less real, man passes
> From unreality to unreality.
> This man [Becket] is obstinate, blind, intent
> On self-destruction,
> Passing from deception to deception,
> From grandeur to grandeur to final illusion.

And a page later the Chorus too cries out from the world of Ernest Hemingway, with also, perhaps, a slight reminiscence of the millrace in *Rosmersholm:*

> We have seen the young man mutilated,
> The torn girl trembling by the mill-stream.
> And meanwhile we have gone on living,
> Living and partly living,
> Picking together the pieces,
> Gathering faggots at nightfall,
> Building a partial shelter,
> For sleeping, and eating and drinking and
>   laughter.

And then, at the very close of part 1, Becket sums up the whole attitude when he turns sharply to address the audience:

> I know
> What yet remains to show you of my history
> Will seem to most of you at best futility,
> Senseless self-slaughter of a lunatic,
> Arrogant passion of a fanatic,
> I know that history at all times draws
> The strangest consequence from remotest cause.

It is exactly the challenge that Shaw has thrown at his readers in the preface to *Saint Joan:* "For us to set up our condition as a standard of sanity, and declare Joan mad because she never condescended to it, is to prove that we are not only lost but irredeemable."

Eliot and Shaw, then, seem to be assuming that the least touch of theology in their plays will serve—to raise a question. And so the saint may become a figure well adapted to arouse something very close to a tragic experience: for here the words sacred, glorious, sacrifice, and the expression in vain may become once again easily appropriate; while at the same time the uncertainty of the audience's attitude—and to some extent the dramatist's own—may enable him to deal also with the painful and pitiful aspects of experience that form the other side of the tragic tension.

But this conflict, this double vision, is not, in these plays, primarily contained within the figure of the saint as tragic hero: Joan and Becket do not here represent humanity in the way of Hamlet or King Oedipus—by focusing within themselves the full tragic tension. They are much more like Oedipus at Colonus, who, although a pitiful beggar in appearance, speaks now through the power of a superhuman insight. Most of his mind lies beyond suffering: he feels that he has found the secret cause, and under the impulse of that cause he moves onward magnificently to his death and transfiguration. The sense of human suffering in *Oedipus at Colonus* is conveyed chiefly in retrospect, or in the sympathetic outcries of the chorus, the weeping of the rejected Polynices, and the anguish of the two daughters whom Oedipus must leave behind.

To see these plays as in any sense tragic it seems that we must abandon the concept of a play built upon an ideal Aristotelian hero and look instead for a tragic experience that arises from the interaction between a hero, who represents the secret cause, and the other characters, who represent the human sufferers. The point is brought out, ironically, by the Archbishop, near the end of Shaw's play, when he warns Joan against the sin of pride, saying, "The old Greek tragedy is rising among us. It is the chastisement of hubris." Joan replies with her usual bluntness, asking, "How can you say that I am disobedient when I always obey my voices, because they come from God." But when the Archbishop insists that "all the voices that come to you are the echoes of your own wilfulness," when he declares angrily, "You stand alone: absolutely alone, trusting to your own conceit, your own ignorance, your own headstrong presumption, your own impiety," we are reminded of Creon berating Oedipus at Colonus, and we are reminded too of Oedipus' long declaration of innocence when Joan turns away, "her eyes skyward," saying, "I have better friends and better counsel than yours."

There is nothing complex about the character of Shaw's Joan; it is the whole fabric of the play that creates something like a tragic tension. For whatever he may say in his preface, Shaw the dramatist, through his huge cast of varied human types, probes the whole range of belief and disbelief in Joan's voices. "They come from your imagination," says the feeble de Baudricourt in the opening scene. "Of course," says Joan, "That is how the messages of God come to us." Cauchon believes the girl to be "inspired, but diabolically inspired." "Many saints have said as much as Joan," Ladvenu suggests. Dunois, her only friend, senses some aura of divinity about her, but becomes extremely uneasy when she talks about her voices. "I should think," he says, "you were a bit cracked if I hadn't noticed that you give me very sensible reasons for what you do, though I hear you telling others you are only obeying Madame Saint Catherine." "Well," she replies, "I have to find reasons for you, because you do not believe in my voices. But the voices come first; and I find the reasons after: whatever you may choose to believe." *Whatever you may choose to believe:* there is the point, and as the figure of Joan flashes onward through the play with only one lapse in confidence—her brief recantation—Shaw keeps his play hovering among choices in a highly modern state of uncertainty: we know and do not know: until at the close Shaw seems to send us over on the side of affirmation. We agree, at least, with the words of the French captain in the opening scene: "There is something about her. . . . Something. . . . I think the girl herself is a bit of a miracle."

She is, as Eliot would say, "a white light still and moving," the simple *cause* of every other word and action in the play; and her absolute simplicity of vision cuts raspingly through all the malign or well-intentioned errors of the world, until in its wrath the world rises up in the form of all its assembled institutions and declares by the voice of all its assembled doctors that this girl is—as Shaw says— *insufferable.*

Thus Joan's apparent resemblance to the Aristotelian hero: her extreme self-confidence, her brashness, her appearance of rash impetuosity—all this becomes in the end a piece of Shavian irony, for her only real error in the play is the one point where her superb self-confidence breaks down in the panic of recantation. And so the hubris is not Joan's but Everyman's. The characters who accuse Joan of pride and error are in those accusations convicting themselves of the pride of self-righteousness and the errors of human certitude. It is true that the suffering that results from this pride and error remains in Shaw's play rather theoretical and remote: and yet we feel it in some degree: in the pallor and anguish of Joan as she resists the temptation to doubt her voices, in the rather unconvincing screams of De Stogumber at the close, and, much more effectively, in the quiet, controlled sympathy of Ladvenu. It would seem, then, that some degree of tragedy resides in this failure of Everyman to recognize absolute Reality, the secret cause, when it appears in the flesh. Must then, cries Cauchon in the epilogue, "Must then a Christ perish in torment in every age to save those that have no imagination?" It is the same symbolism that Eliot has evoked in the beginning of his play, where the Chorus asks: "Shall the Son of Man be born again in the litter of scorn?"

We need not be too greatly concerned with Shaw's bland assertions that he is letting us in on the truth about the Middle Ages, telling us in the play all we need to know about Joan. Books and articles have appeared—a whole cloudburst of them—devoted to proving that Shaw's methods of historical research in his play and in his preface are open to serious question. But Shaw gave that game away long ago when he announced: "I deal with all periods; but I never study any period but the present, which I have not yet mastered and never shall"; or when he said, with regard to Cleopatra's cure for Caesar's baldness, that his methods of scholarship, as compared with Gilbert Murray's, consisted in "pure divination." The preface to *Saint Joan* lays down a long barrage of historicity, which in the end is revealed as a remarkable piece of Shavio-Swiftian hoaxing: for in the last few pages of that long preface he adds, incidentally, that his use of the "available documentation" has been accompanied by "such powers of divination as I possess"; he concedes that for some figures in his play he has invented "appropriate characters" "in Shakespear's manner"; and that, fundamentally, his play is built upon what he calls "the inevitable flatteries of tragedy." That is, there is no historical basis for his highly favorable characterizations of Cauchon and the Inquisitor, upon which the power and point of the trial scene are founded.

I do not mean to say, however, that our sense of history is irrelevant to an appreciation of Shaw's play. There is a point to be made by considering such a book as J. M. Robertson's *Mr. Shaw and*

"The Maid," which complains bitterly, upon historical grounds, against Shaw's "instinct to put things both ways." This is a book, incidentally, which Eliot has praised very highly because it points out that in this kind of subject "Facts matter," and that "to Mr. Shaw, truth and falsehood . . . do not seem to have the same meaning as to ordinary people." But the point lies rather in the tribute that such remarks pay to the effectiveness of Shaw's realistic dramaturgy.

Shaw is writing, as he and Ibsen had to write, within the conventions of the modern realistic theater—conventions which Eliot escaped in *Murder in the Cathedral* because he was writing this play for performance at the Canterbury Festival. But in his later plays, composed for the theater proper, Eliot has also been forced to, at least he has chosen to, write within these stern conventions.

Now in the realistic theater, as Francis Fergusson has suggested, the artist seems to be under the obligation to pretend that he is not an artist at all but is simply interested in pursuing the truth "in some pseudo-scientific sense." Thus we find the relation of art to life so often driven home on the modern stage by such deep symbolic actions as removing the cubes from ice trays or cooking an omelette for dinner. Shaw knows that on this stage facts matter—or at least the appearance of facts—and in this need for a dramatic realism lies the basic justification for Shaw's elaborately argued presentation of Joan as a Protestant and nationalist martyr killed by the combined institutional forces of feudalism and the Church. Through these historical theories, developed within the body of the play, Joan is presented as the agent of a transformation in the actual world; the theories have enough plausibility for dramatic purposes, and perhaps a bit more; this, together with Shaw's adaptation of the records of Joan's trial, gives him all the "facts" that he needs to make his point in the modern theater.

Some of Joan's most Shavian remarks are in fact her own words as set down in the long records of her trial: as, for example, where her questioner asks whether Michael does not appear to her as a naked man. "Do you think God cannot afford clothes for him?" answers Joan, in the play and in the records. Shaw has made a skillful selection of these answers, using, apparently, the English translation of the documents edited by Douglas Murray; and he has set these answers together with speeches of his own modeled upon their tone and manner. In this way he has been able to bring within the limits of the realistic theater the very voice that rings throughout these trial records, the voice of the lone girl fencing with, stabbing at, baffling, and defeating the crowd of some sixty learned men: a voice that is not speaking within the range of the other voices that assail her. Thus we hear her in the following speech adapted from half a dozen places in the records: "I have said again and again that I will tell you all that concerns this trial. But I cannot tell you the whole truth: God does not allow the whole truth to be told. . . . It is an old saying that he who tells too much truth is sure to be hanged. . . . I have sworn as much as I will swear; and I will swear no more." Or, following the documents much more closely, her answers thus resound when the questioners attempt to force her to submit her case to the Church on earth: "I will obey The Church," says Joan, "provided it does not command anything impossible."

> If you command me to declare that all that I have done and said, and all the visions and revelations I have had, were not from God, then that is impossible: I will not declare it for anything in the world. What God made me do I will never go back on; and what He has commanded or shall command I will not fail to do in spite of any man alive. That is what I mean by impossible. And in case The Church should bid me do anything contrary to the command I have from God, I will not consent to it, no matter what it may be.

In thus maintaining the tone of that—extraordinary—voice, Shaw has, I think, achieved an effect that is in some ways very close to the effect of the "intersection of the timeless with time," which Eliot has achieved in his play, and which he has described in "The Dry Salvages":

> Men's curiosity searches past and future
> And clings to that dimension. But to apprehend
> The point of intersection of the timeless
> With time, is an occupation for the saint—
> No occupation either, but something given
> And taken, in a lifetime's death in love,
> Ardour and selflessness and self-surrender.

An obvious similarity between the two plays may be seen in the tone of satirical wit that runs through both—notably in the ludicrous prose speeches that Eliot's murdering Knights deliver to the audience in self-defense. These have an essentially Shavian purpose: "to shock the audience out of their complacency," as Eliot has recently said, going on to admit, "I may, for aught I know, have been slightly under the influence of *St. Joan*" (*Poetry and Drama*). The atmosphere of wit is evident also in the first part of Eliot's play, in the cynical attitude of the Herald who announces Becket's return:

> The streets of the city will be packed to suffocation,
> And I think that his horse will be deprived of its tail,
> A single hair of which becomes a precious relic.

Or, more important, in the speeches of the Four Tempters, who match the Four Knights of part 2, and who tend to speak, as the Knights also do in places, in a carefully calculated doggerel that betrays their fundamental shallowness:

> I leave you to the pleasures of your higher vices,
> Which will have to be paid for at higher prices.
> Farewell, my Lord, I do not wait upon ceremony,
> I leave as I came, forgetting all acrimony,
> Hoping that your present gravity
> Will find excuse for my humble levity.
> If you will remember me, my Lord, at your prayers,
> I'll remember you at kissing-time below the stairs.

In all these ways Eliot, like Shaw, maintains his action in the "real" world: and by other means as well. By keeping before us the central question of our own time: "Is it war or peace?" asks Eliot's priest. "Peace," replies the Herald, "but not the kiss of peace. / A patched up affair, if you ask my opinion." By the frequently realistic imagery of the Chorus, made up of "the scrubbers and sweepers of Canterbury." By the frequent use in part 2 of the recorded words that passed between Becket and the Knights in the year 1170. By throwing our minds back to the literary forms of the Middle Ages: to *Everyman,* from which Eliot has taken a good many hints for the tone and manner of Becket's encounter with the Tempters, and which, as he says, he has kept in mind as a model for the versification of his dialogue. To this last we should also add a special device of heavy alliteration (particularly notable in the Second Temptation), which seems to work in two ways: it reminds us of the English alliterative verse of the Middle Ages, and thus gives the play a further

historical focus, and it also suggests here a rhetoric of worldly ambition in keeping with the temptation that Becket is undergoing:

> Think, my lord,
> Power obtained grows to glory,
> Life lasting, a permanent possession,
> A templed tomb, monument of marble.
> Rule over men reckon no madness.

Both Eliot and Shaw, then, have in their own ways taken pains to
place their action simultaneously in the "real" past and the "real"
present: an action firmly fixed in time must underlie the shock of
intersection.

But of course in Eliot's play the cause of intersection, the agent
of transformation, the saint, is utterly different from Shaw's, and
thus the plays become, so obviously, different. Shaw's Joan is the
active saint, operating in the world; Eliot's Becket is a contemplative
figure, ascetic, "withdrawn to contemplation," holding within his
mind, and reconciling there alone, the stresses of the world. His
immobility is his strength; he is the still point, the center of the world
that moves about him, as his sermon is the center of the play.

One is struck here by the similarity between the total conception
of Eliot's play and of *Oedipus at Colonus*. Both heroes, after a long
period of wandering, have found, at their entrance, their place of rest
and their place of death in a sacred spot: Becket in his Cathedral,
Oedipus in the sacred wood of the Furies or Eumenides. Both heroes
maintain the attitude that Oedipus states at the outset: "Nevermore
will I depart from my rest in this land." Both reveal in their opening
speeches the view that, as Oedipus says, "patience is the lesson of
suffering." Both are then subjected to various kinds of temptations
to leave the spot; both are forced to recapitulate their past while
enduring these trials; both remain immobile, unmovable; both win a
glorious death and by that death benefit the land in which they die.
Both are surrounded by a large cast of varied human sufferers, who
do not understand the saint, who try to deflect him from his ways,
and who in some cases mourn his loss bitterly: the cry of Eliot's
priest at the end is like the cries of Antigone and Ismene:

> O father, father, gone from us, lost to us,
> How shall we find you, from what far place
> Do you look down on us?

I suspect that *Oedipus at Colonus* has in fact had a deep and early influence upon Eliot's whole career: "Sweeney among the Nightingales" alludes to this very wood, which Sophocles' chorus describes as a place where

> The sweet, sojourning nightingale
> Murmurs all day long. . . .
>
> And here the choiring Muses come,
> And the divinity of love
> With the gold reins in her hand.

The fact that the Muses haunt this wood may throw some light too upon the title of Eliot's first book of essays, *The Sacred Wood,* the book in which he revealed his early interest in the possibility of a poetic drama.

But our main point here is the way in which this deeply religious tragedy of Sophocles, which had already provided a strong formative precedent for Milton's *Samson Agonistes,* now provides us with a precedent for regarding Eliot's saint's play as a tragedy. The precedent may also explain why a strong coloring of Greek-like fatalism runs throughout Eliot's Christian play: a coloring which some of Eliot's critics have found disturbing. But these classical reminiscences of Destiny and Fate and Fortune's wheel remind us only of the base upon which Eliot is building: they do not delimit his total meaning. We can see this amalgamation of Greek and Christian at work in Becket's opening speech—the most important speech of the play, which all the rest of the play explores and illustrates. It is the speech which Becket's Fourth Tempter, his inmost self, repeats in mockery, word for word, twenty pages later and thus suggests that these Temptations—of pleasure, worldly power, and spiritual pride—are to be regarded as fundamentally a recapitulation of the stages by which Becket has reached the state of mind he displays at his entrance. He believes that he has found a secret cause, and he enters prepared to die in that belief: "Peace," he says to the worried priest, and then, referring to the Chorus of anxious women, continues:

> They speak better than they know, and beyond your
>   understanding.
> They know and do not know, what it is to act or
>   suffer.

They know and do not know, that acting is
    suffering
And suffering is action. Neither does the actor suffer
Nor the patient act. But both are fixed
In an eternal action, an eternal patience
To which all must consent that it may be willed
And which all must suffer that they may will it,
That the pattern may subsist, for the pattern is the
    action
And the suffering, that the wheel may turn and still
Be forever still.

We can worry about the ambiguities of those words "suffering" and "patient" as long as we wish: in the end Becket keeps his secret almost as stubbornly as Joan or Oedipus:

I have had a tremor of bliss, a wink of heaven, a whisper,
And I would no longer be denied; all things
Proceed to a joyful consummation.

But halfway between these two passages lies Becket's Christmas sermon, presented as a four-page interlude between the play's two parts. It is one of the most surprisingly successful moments in the modern theater, for who would expect to find a sermon, and an interesting sermon, here? It owes its success to an atmosphere of restrained and controlled mystery and to the fact that it is not really an interlude at all, but a deep expression of the play's central theme, binding the play's two parts into one. Becket is speaking of this word *Peace,* the word that dominates the play, for all the actors and sufferers in the play are seeking peace, on their own terms. But the meaning of the word for Becket is conveyed only obliquely, by Becket's tone, his poise, his humility, his acceptance, "Thus devoted, concentrated in purpose." He can display only by his own action and suffering what this word Peace means to him, for he is trying to explain the meaning of the unspoken Word that lies locked in the visible and verbal paradoxes of acting and suffering.

And only in this way, too, can Becket display that submission of the will by which he avoids the final temptation of spiritual pride. The Temptations make it clear that Becket has been a proud man— even an arrogant man: the first priest, the Tempters, and the Knights all accuse him, with some reason, of pride. And we hear him speaking at times throughout the play, and even at the very end, in a harsh, acid tone, which here and there is uncomfortably close to condescension. Eliot's control of the character is not perhaps as firm as we could wish, though there is nothing that a skillful actor cannot handle, for the central conception is clear: like Oedipus, Becket is still a man, and retains the marks of his natural character: but in the sermon we grasp his saintliness.

At the same time Becket conveys to us the essence of the view of Tragedy that we are here considering. Becket's sermon ponders the fact that in the services of Christmas the Church celebrates birth and death simultaneously. Now, "as the World sees," Becket says, "this is to behave in a strange fashion. For who in the World will both mourn and rejoice at once and for the same reason?" And this is true on other occasions, he adds: "so also, in a smaller figure, we both rejoice and mourn in the death of martyrs. We mourn, for the sins of the world that has martyred them; we rejoice, that another soul is numbered among the Saints."

It is this tension, this double vision, that Eliot presents in his great choral odes. What Eliot has done is to allow everyone in his play except the Chorus and Becket to remain the simplest possible types—simpler even than Shaw's: ciphers who serve their functions: to provide an outline of the action and a setting for the problem. Into the cries of the Chorus he has poured the tragic experience of suffering humanity, caught in the grip of a secret cause: "We are forced to bear witness."

The Chorus opens the play with fear and reluctance and hopelessness, asking who it is who shall

> Stretch out his hand to the fire, and deny his master?
>   who shall be warm
> By the fire, and deny his master?

They know and do not know who it is—themselves—bending to the earth like animals seeking their protective coloring:

> Now I fear disturbance of the quiet seasons:
> Winter shall come bringing death from the sea,
> Ruinous spring shall beat at our doors,
> Root and shoot shall eat our eyes and our ears,
> Disastrous summer burn up the beds of our streams
> And the poor shall wait for another decaying October.

These dead do not desire resurrection; and when their Lord Arch-bishop reappears to them, they can only cry out, "O Thomas, re-turn, Archbishop; return, return to France. . . . Leave us to perish in quiet." They would like to go on "living and partly living," like Shaw's Dauphin, who irritably shies away from Joan, saying, "I want to sleep in a comfortable bed." Eliot's Chorus starts from this point—by the fireside and the bed—a point which Shaw's chorus of varied actors hardly goes beyond. But Eliot's Chorus moves far beyond this point, undergoing what Kenneth Burke or Francis Fergusson might call a ritual of transformation. They are not at all the "foolish, immodest and babbling women," which Eliot's priest calls them, but the heart of humanity moving under the impulse of a half-realized cause. Under this impulse they have moved, by the end of part 1, into the range of a "stifling scent of despair," which nevertheless is not spreading blindly outwards: for the Chorus

> The forms take shape in the dark air:
> Puss-purr of leopard, footfall of padding bear,
> Palm-pat of nodding ape, square hyaena waiting
> For laughter, laughter, laughter. The Lords of Hell are
> here.

But after Becket's sermon the Chorus has taken some heart: they no longer seem to fear the spring:

> When the leaf is out on the tree, when the elder and may
> Burst over the stream, and the air is clear and high,
> And voices trill at windows, and children tumble in
> front of the door,
> What work shall have been done, what wrong
> Shall the bird's song cover, the green tree cover, what
> wrong
> Shall the fresh earth cover?

From this oscillation between despair and a half-hope arises the play's greatest poetry, as the Chorus moves on far out of the range of ordinary fears and hopes into a nightmare vision that renews and extends the animal imagery and the dense imagery of taste and smell and the other senses, by which the Chorus had expressed its horror at the close of part 1; but now there is more than horror: the Chorus is moving on here to a vision of humanity's living relation with all being, to a sense that all of creation from the worm to the Prince is involved in this sacrifice:

> I have smelt them, the death-bringers, senses are
>   quickened
> By subtile forebodings . . .
>   I have tasted
> The savour of putrid flesh in the spoon. I have felt
> The heaving of earth at nightfall, restless, absurd.
>   I have heard
> Laughter in the noises of beasts that make strange
>   noises . . .
>   I have eaten
> Smooth creatures still living, with the strong salt
>   taste of living things under sea . . .
>   In the air
> Flirted with the passage of the kite, I have plunged
>   with the kite and cowered with the
>   wren. . . .
>   I have seen
> Rings of light coiling downwards, leading
> To the horror of the ape. . . .
> I have consented, Lord Archbishop, have
>   consented.

Beyond this recognition of responsibility for the action and the suffering, there lies a step into the vision of ultimate horror which they face just before the murder: a vision of utter spiritual death: the Dark Night of the Soul:

> Emptiness, absence, separation from God;
> The horror of the effortless journey, to the empty land
> Which is no land, only emptiness, absence, the Void.

This, paradoxically, is their moment of deepest vision, of greatest courage; the point at which they fully comprehend their need for the sacrifice about to be permitted, suffered, and which provides the answer to their cries during the very act of the murder: "Clear the air! clean the sky! wash the wind! take the stone from the stone, take the skin from the arm, take the muscle from the bone, and wash them. Wash the stone, wash the bone, wash the brain, wash the soul, wash them wash them!" Like King Oedipus they are, without quite realizing it, being washed in this "rain of blood" that is blinding their eyes.

As these cries from the conscience of humanity fade away, the lights fade out—and then come on again in the foreground with a glaring brightness—as the four Murderers step forward, make their bows, and present their ridiculous speeches of defense—in the manner of an after-dinner speaker: "I knew Becket well, in various official relations; and I may say that I have never known a man so well qualified for the highest rank of the Civil Service." Or in the manner of the parliamentary orator: "I must repeat one point that the last speaker has made. While the late Archbishop was Chancellor, he wholeheartedly supported the King's designs: this is an important point, which, if necessary, I can substantiate." Or in the manner of the brisk attorney: "I think, with these facts before you, you will unhesitatingly render a verdict of Suicide while of Unsound Mind."

The lights fade out again, the Knights disappear, and then gradually the lights come on once more to reveal the priests and the Chorus in their old positions. It is as if the Knights had never spoken: the conscience of humanity has been working deep within while the Knights were speaking on the surface, and now the Chorus sums up its discoveries, its transformation, in a psalm of praise, in which once again it affirms a union with the whole creation, but this time in a tone of joy and peace:

> We praise Thee, O God, for Thy glory displayed in all
> the creatures of the earth,
> In the snow, in the rain, in the wind, in the storm; in
> all of Thy creatures, both the hunters and the
> hunted. . . .
> They affirm Thee in living; all things affirm Thee in
> living; the bird in the air, both the hawk and
> the finch; the beast on the earth, both the
> wolf and the lamb; the worm in the soil and
> the worm in the belly. . . .
> Even in us the voices of seasons, the snuffle of winter,
> the song of spring, the drone of summer, the
> voices of beasts and of birds, praise Thee.

Those words from the final chorus may remind us again of the long tentacles of correlated imagery that reach throughout these choral odes: imagery of beasts and birds and worms; of seasons, of violent death, of the daily hardships of the partly living life: with the result that these choral odes grow together into a long poem, interwoven with verse and prose pitched at a lower intensity; and by this interweaving of the odes, even more than by Becket, the play is drawn into unity.

We can see now the effect that these different manifestations of a secret cause have had upon the total construction of our two saint's plays. Eliot's play, focused on a contemplative saint, displays what we might call a semicircular structure: with Becket as the still center and the Chorus sweeping out around him in a broad dramatic action, a poetical ballet of transformation. Shaw's play, based on an active saint, develops instead a linear structure, as of a spear driving straight for the mark. It is marred, here and there, by irrelevant or maladjusted witticisms, and the whole character of De Stogumber is a misfortune. Yet Joan and her voices seem to work like key symbols in a poem: appearing in a carefully designed sequence of different contexts: six scenes, with six differing moods, moving from farce to high comedy, to a romantic glimpse of the warrior Joan in shining armor, and from here into an area of deepening somberness, until, by the fifth scene, the world of Shaw's play, too, has been transformed—from the foolish to the tragic. Now we have in his play, too, the dim silence of the Cathedral, with Joan praying symbolically before the Stations of the Cross: her white raiment revealing the saint whose mission is now nearly complete. The king is crowned; she has shown France how to win; and now, as her allies, one by one, and even Dunois, fail to answer the unbearable demands of the superhuman, Joan goes forth to meet the cheering crowd who will kiss her garments and line her roadway with palms. The way is now prepared for the massive trial scene, the tragic agon, which presents what Eliot calls "a symbol perfected in death."

And then, the epilogue. Many have found this a disconcerting, inartistic mixture of farce, satire, and didactic explanation. I agree. But I do not see why the epilogue should spoil the play. An epilogue is no part of the dramatic action: it is the author's chance to step forward, relaxed and garrulous, and to talk the play over with the audience. Traditionally, it is true, the epilogue is recited by only one performer—by Prospero, for instance. There is a slight difference here: Shaw has had his entire cast recite the epilogue. But it is still appended commentary on the action, not a part of the action. Moreover, this kind of thing is not without precedent in performances of tragedy. The ancient Greeks appear to have liked exactly this kind of release in their festivals of tragedy, since they demanded that each dramatist, after presenting his three tragedies, should provide them with their satyr-play, usually of an uproarious and ribald variety, sometimes burlesquing elements of the very story that had just been seen in tragic dignity. The epilogue is Shaw's satyr-play: a bursting forth of that strong sense of the ridiculous which Shaw has, during the play proper, subjected to a remarkable control—remarkable, that is, for Shaw.

It seems possible, then, to find some place, within the spacious area of tragedy, for our two saint's plays. It seems possible, if we will not demand an Aristotelian hero, and if we may view the area of tragedy as a sort of scale or spectrum ranging between the two poles of doubt and affirmation: or, to put it more precisely, between the pole of fruitless suffering and the pole of universal cause. Not a scale of value, but a spectrum of various qualities, with *A Farewell to Arms* marking one extreme, outside the area of tragedy, and Shakespeare's *Tempest,* perhaps, marking the other extreme. In between, within the area of tragedy, would lie an enormous variety of works that would defy any rigorous attempt at definition, except that all would show in some degree a mingled atmosphere of doubt and affirmation, of human suffering and secret cause. Far over toward the side of fruitless suffering we might find the plays of Ibsen, or *Othello;* somewhere in the middle, *Hamlet,* or *Oedipus Rex;* and far over toward the other side we might find a triad of strongly affirmative tragedies: *Oedipus at Colonus, Samson Agonistes,* and *Murder in the Cathedral;* and still farther over, perhaps hanging on by his hands to the very rim of tragedy—we might even find a place for Bernard Shaw.

A Hagiography of Creative Evolution

Louis Crompton

Back to Methuselah is not only a dramatic essay on politics and biology. It also provides the iconography, as Shaw called it, for the religion Don Juan first preached in the hell scene of *Man and Superman*. Adam's fall, in Shaw's interpretation of the Eden story, is due to his original sin of negligence, that is, to his failure to exercise his will effectively once his limited life span gave him only a limited interest in the future. From his failure of will and from Cain's desire for self-aggrandisement spring the social evils of idleness, violence, and exploitation. After presenting the fall in this new perspective, Shaw first announces a new gospel, and then shows us a new elect who are biologically redeemed from the fallen state of man. Finally, the ministers of godhead triumph over matter, death, and evil. Shaw did not, however, find virtue only in the future: man's present corrupt state did not preclude the appearance from time to time of exceptional individuals who constitute an order of sainthood. It is logical, then, that Shaw, having dramatized a new body of myth for his religion of Creative Evolution in one set of plays, should next have undertaken to write a chapter of its hagiography.

For his subject Shaw chose Joan of Arc. But why did he pick this particular medieval saint? Perhaps we may best see what Shaw is about if we look at his play in the light of the philosophy of history. John Stuart Mill, following the French critic Saint-Simon, has pointed out that ages of faith and of doubt have tended to succeed each other

From *Shaw the Dramatist*. © 1969 by the University of Nebraska Press.

historically. Nowhere is this theory better borne out than in the historiography of Joan. No one has ever been more trenchantly debunked or more piously exalted. Rationalistic ages have deprecated her, while the alternating ages of faith have reaffirmed their belief in her greatness. To see the contrast clearly we need only set Voltaire's portrait of Joan side by side with Schiller's or Southey's: the eighteenth century, which laughed at saints and heroes, pooh-poohed her, while the nineteenth century put her back on a pedestal. On the one hand we have a hilarious spoofing of her story, on the other a spurious romantic idealization.

Shaw's relation to these various currents of faith and skepticism is by no means simple, since he was at the same time the spiritual heir of the Enlightenment and of the transcendental reaction against it. Among his intellectual forebears are both Voltaire, the mocker, and Carlyle, the arch-anti-*philosophe.* He shared with the utilitarians both their distrust of moral traditions based on mere custom or taboo, and their determination to take a hard look at the practical consequences of human actions quite apart from high motives and good intentions. But though he found the negative weapons of utilitarian criticism useful for demolishing dead ideals, he is not, in a positive sense, a utilitarian at all, since he rejects both their rationalistic logic and their hedonist ethics. When it comes to beliefs and values, he is, on the contrary, a Platonist, an apriorist, an antipragmatist, and a mystic.

Mill thought the best of all worlds would combine the free critical spirit of a skeptical age with the coherent convictions and fervor of an age of "organic" faith. Shaw's *Saint Joan* is an attempt to achieve a Millite synthesis through the evaluation of one remarkable historical figure. If we want to understand the play we must be aware of how these two opposing currents mingle in it and find their resolution. To take two points on each side of the balance: in its rejection of supernaturalism and its indictment of orthodoxy (as embodied in the Inquisition), *Saint Joan* is an infidel drama; in its view of Joan's visions as superratiocinative and its celebration of her mystic sainthood, it belongs to the tradition of faith.

Shaw read scores of writers on Joan. He mentions at least a dozen by name—Shakespeare, Voltaire, Schiller, Michelet, Henri Martin, Henri Wallon, Marcel Poullin, Mark Twain, Tom Taylor, Percy MacKaye, Anatole France, and Andrew Lang. Their writings include, respectively, a political melodrama, a mock-heroic poem, a tragedy, four historical studies, a novel, two more plays, and two critical biographies. Most of these works fit clearly into one or the other of the infidel and the fideist traditions. The one exception is the play by Shakespeare—or whoever was responsible for the disputed authorship of *Henry VI, Part I*. Here the playwright violates the general rule that the fideist plays are favorable to Joan and the infidel ones critical of her and her admirers. The author clearly believes in Joan, but he believes in her as the agent of diabolical, not of heavenly, powers. Reflecting the scurrilous popular Anglo-Burgundian estimate of Joan current in England until the seventeenth century and most accessible to Elizabethan readers in the pages of Holinshed's *Chronicles,* the play treats Joan as a harlot-witch who owes her victories to the devil. Yet even this melodrama cannot be said to be without influence on Shaw, for he takes the anti-Joan bias that runs throughout and ascribes it to his English chaplain, De Stogumber.

The most influential debunking works on Joan have been Voltaire's *La Pucelle* (ca. 1730) and Anatole France's *Vie de Jeanne d'Arc* (1908). Voltaire's poem is less an attempt to write history than an exuberant exercise in anticlericalism. Voltaire is above all else interested in poking fun at miracle-mongering, saint-worship, and belief in the magical powers of virginity as they persisted into the age of reason. While anti-Joan sentiment lingered in England, a pro-Joan cult had grown up in France, carefully fostered by the clergy as a prop to popular religion. To counter this, Voltaire impishly turns Joan into a bouncing chambermaid whose seduction is the chief aim of English strategy. Ribald, satirical, and wildly extravagant at every turn, Voltaire has no compunction about departing from history by marrying Joan off to Dunois and ending his poem with their wedding. Antaole France's biography, by contrast, is a model of scholarly sobriety, completely free from Voltaire's comic and erotic license. Yet for all its difference in tone and method, it is still the work of a man who is patently grinding the same axes. France is reacting against Joan's nineteenth-century rehabilitation as Voltaire reacted against her seventeenth- and eighteenth-century cult. Nor, though France (like Voltaire) is sympathetic to Joan as a person, does he believe in her greatness. From his skeptical point of view her visions are simply hysterical hallucinations, her mission a priestly stratagem to increase the prestige of the Church in the national struggle, and her military prowess a mere legend grown up around a simple young girl who was no more than the army's mascot.

Shaw's play is not without its Voltairism, particularly in its treatment of popular credulity. Moreover, though he gives us dignified churchmen who are models of personal integrity rather than absurd figures of fun, Shaw is not, in the last analysis, one whit less antiecclesiastical. Shaw's basic approach, however, is distinctly closer to the line of mid-nineteenth-century French liberal historians, of whom Jules Michelet was the most important. These writers, though outside the Church, were much more sympathetic to the Middle Ages and to Joan's messianic side than the *philosophes* had been. Yet Shaw is as critical of several aspects of nineteenth-century Johannamania as he was of Voltaire and France. He especially decried the tendency to make Joan a romantic heroine or a melodramatic victim. Here Schiller and Mark Twain struck him as the prime offenders. Schiller wrote *Die Jungfrau von Orleans* (1801) as a corrective to Voltaire's farcical irreverence. In it, Joan is a lyrically eloquent warrior-prophetess, torn between patriotism and love for an enemy soldier. Her amorous dilemma, and the fact that Schiller's Maid dies, not at the stake, but on the battlefield, removes her story as far from history in the direction of high romance as Voltaire's mock-epic does in the direction of freewheeling satire. Shaw praised *Die Jungfrau* as a "tender and beautiful picture" but complained that Schiller had idealized Joan out of all recognition. Nor did Mark Twain's serious fictionalized biography, purportedly the memoirs of Joan's page, please him better. Twain's book is sympathetic melodrama, or *Henry VI* turned upside down. His *Personal Recollections of Joan of Arc* (1896) transforms Joan into a sweetly pathetic child saint, surrounded by ugly monsters. Cauchon is an obese butcher, so that Joan's relation to him is not unlike Little Nell's to Quilp. And though Twain is not antipathetic to Catholicism, he is intensely hostile to the fifteenth century, which he denounces as the "brutallest" and "rottenest" era since the Dark Ages.

Depictions of Joan on the English stage were no novelty before Shaw. Two versions he was personally familiar with were those of Tom Taylor, the Victorian dramatist, and Percy MacKaye, a contemporary American littérateur. Taylor's *Joan of Arc* (1871) was a popular melodrama not far removed from Twain in spirit, with a suborned spy in place of Cauchon as the stage villain. Then in 1902 an even occurred which put English-language treatments of Joan's story on a new footing. In that year T. Douglas Murray published a full translation of Quicherat's transcriptions of the trial of 1431 and the rehabilitation proceedings of 1456 under the title *Jeanne d'Arc, Maid of Orleans, Deliverer of France: Being the Story of Her Life, Her Achievements and Her Death, as Attested on Oath and Set Forth in the Original Documents.* Later, this translation was to become the immediate source for Shaw's own play, but in the meantime Mrs. Patrick Campbell drew MacKaye's attention to it as possible material for the stage. The resulting drama, *Jeanne d'Arc* (1906), belongs, like Shaw's, to the literary tradition of English Pre-Raphaelitism. But MacKaye's Pre-Raphaelitism is not of the vigorous Shavian sort; rather it is Yeatsian—that is, poetically romantic and picturesque. MacKaye's Joan is no robust farm girl, but a recognizable cousin of Yeats's wistful Countess Cathleen, and like the latter, a great breaker of hearts. The play's highly self-conscious neomedievalism, though very pretty, is far from the rough realism of the popular medieval stage. After watching Julia Marlowe perform the title role, Shaw remarked that MacKaye's heroine was "pitiable, sentimental, and in the technical melodramatic sense, 'sympathetic' " and about as much like Joan "as Joan's kitten was like Joan's charger."

After all this abuse, adulation, bawdry, debunking, melodrama, and romance, the reader may be tempted to exclaim skeptically, "Tot homines, tot Johannae," and to decide that men have simply recreated Joan from age to age after their own image. Obviously, to write about Joan is, like writing about Christ, to reveal not only one's religious beliefs, but also one's conception of the possibilities and limits of human life itself. It is also to reveal one's views on sainthood and heroism, on the capacities of women, and on the political and historical forces that shape society. Shaw, in writing *Saint Joan,* had all these matters in mind.

We may begin with Joan's sainthood, since from among the multitude of epithets bestowed on her by friend and foe, Shaw has chosen "Saint" for his title. His choice was not simply a way of pointing up the irony of the Church's turnabout at her canonization in 1920. Traditionally, saints, in the orthodox ecclesiastical sense of the word, have been distinguished from other men by their miracle-working, by their self-mortification, and by their expiatory martyrdoms, which have been regarded as contributing to a vicarious treasury of merit for mankind. All of these notions of sainthood Shaw emphatically rejects. Far from countenancing supernaturalism, Shaw treats miracles as satirically as Voltaire and France do. He is even more adamant on the subject of self-mortification. While

Schopenhauer had praised Christian above Greek tragedy on the ground that the Christian saint negates his will, "joyfully forsaking the world," Shaw, who does not share Schopenhauer's belief in human depravity, thinks man is saved by affirming his will, not by negating it. Joan's triumph lies just in this—her assertion of her will—and the pride which the Archbishop, looking at her from the Greco-Christian point of view, denounces as *hubris* is for Shaw the source of her salvation—pride and its concomitant, self-respect, being exactly what the Dauphin, the court, and the French ecclesiastics have been lacking.

As to the horrific side of martyrdom—the side which has always made the greatest appeal to the popular imagination—Shaw considers it on exactly the same level with the attraction of grisly tragedies reported in sensational newspapers. When he gave a radio speech in 1931 on the five hundredth anniversary of her death, he begged his audience to forget Joan had ever been burned. Furthermore, he strongly condemned the moral theory that regarded such deaths as expiatory sacrifices. Strangely enough, even liberal historians have been tinged with such notions: Michelet, though strongly in reaction against clericalism, nevertheless imagined Joan as longing for a "purifying death." This stupid attitude, which finds something morally efficacious in torture, so tried Shaw's patience that on one occasion he was moved to cry out in exasperation that he hated the cross as he hated all gibbets.

Yet sainthood is for Shaw something more than the mere absurdity it was for Voltaire and Anatole France. For all his unorthodoxy, Shaw is a man who looks at the world primarily in theological terms, and the epithet of his title makes a serious claim for Joan's eligibility in a Shavian "Communion of Saints," whose canon, including as it does non-Christians like Socrates and Mahomet and even professed atheists like Shelley is more catholic than the canon of Catholicism. Carlyle also speaks of a "Communion of Saints" in this broader sense, and Shaw follows the Carlylean tradition further in calling the power which moves Joan miraculous and mystical, since, though it is not supernatural, it is nevertheless superpersonal and outside the realm of logic or reason. In so doing, he equates the life force, or evolutionary appetite, with what a theologian would call the will of God. Joan's suffering is holy, not as an expiation, but because it is the consequence of her struggle to advance the race, and as such is "the food of godhead." Obviously, such a view of Joan was calculated to provoke dissent from rationalists and orthodox Christians in equal measure. It is not, then, at all paradoxical that a churchgoer like T. S. Eliot should have applauded what he called the "steamrollering" of Shaw by J. M. Robertson, the arch-rationalist, in the latter's *Mr. Shaw and "The Maid."* Indeed, Shaw must have considered Eliot's attack on his play from the orthodox position a high compliment, since it implied that he had recognized that, in *Saint Joan,* a live religion was at work competing for men's souls with his own Anglo-Catholicism. In this light, Eliot's own *Murder in the Cathedral* can be regarded as an attempt to reaffirm the ecclesiastical ideal of sainthood in reply to Shaw's challenge.

Skeptical historians have not only denied the religious nature of Joan's inspiration; they have also cast doubt on her prowess as a warrior. Shaw's preface and play take direct issue here with Anatole France, who simply refused to credit the possibility that an uneducated girl in her teens could have acted as an effective military leader. Robertson, in his turn, accused Shaw of falling back on mere "historic polemic" in making his claims for Joan. But whether or not this is the case may be seen by turning to the record of sworn testimony at the rehabilitation trial. Here the French general, Alençon, though he stresses Joan's naïveté in other matters, speaks of the amazement he felt on discovering that "for warlike things—bearing the lance, assembling an army, ordering military operations, directing artillery—she was most skillful." Dunois, too, states quite as unequivocally that Joan "executed many marvelous manoeuvres which had not been thought of by two or three accomplished generals working together." Since the aim of the rehabilitation proceedings was specifically to establish Joan's sanctity and piety in order to clear her of the charge of witchcraft, and since any evidence as to her military ability was, so to speak, gratuitous, and even detrimental to the view that her victories were chiefly the result of divine favor, we may safely trust the record at this point and assume that, for all his trenchancy, Robertson is here simply indulging in skepticism for skepticism's sake.

Having shorn Joan's legend of its supernaturalism and her death of its mystery as a ritual atonement, Shaw was also determined to remove the accretions of popular romance. This meant de-eroticizing Joan and desentimentalizing her. Before Shaw, nearly every literary man who had dealt with her story added some sexual element for dramatic interest: Shakespeare gives her the baleful attractiveness of a villainess in a spy novel, Voltaire a luscious nubility, Schiller a broken heart, and Mark Twain a winsomeness capable of engaging male sympathies at a glance. Shaw, by denying that Joan had any "touching and charming love affairs" and by citing her comrades' testimony on her lack of sex appeal, broke radically with the traditions of literary history. His Joan is not a soft woman who melts men's hearts, but a bossy one who stirs them. His models were not the heroines of romance, but the militant leaders of the woman's suffrage movement in the first decades of the twentieth century. To this force of will he adds a peasant directness of expression which is surely closer to the mark than the chivalry Andrew Lang and the Renaissance romance writers ascribe to her. Indeed, if one reads her letters, there is more of the style of Khrushchev in them than of Chaucer's "parfit gentil knight." There she reveals herself, as in Shaw's play, as a woman lacking both aristocratic suavity and middle-class caution but amply endowed with courage, blunt vigor, and common sense.

Shaw's endorsement of Joan's nationalism is perhaps more surprising. In this matter he was anticipated by Schiller, who, moved by embryonic pan-Germanism, made Joan not merely a French patriot, but a champion of nationalism per se. But Shaw, after all, deprecated national self-determination as an ultimate good in itself; on the contrary, he held that it was a positive advantage for small, barbaric countries to be conquered by larger, more civilized ones. Yet though Shaw was an internationalist rather than a romantic nationalist in politics, he also believed that it was a law of history that countries should pass through a nationalist phase as part of their organic development:

> Here, then, we have to face an inevitable order of social growth. First, the individual will have his personal liberty, in pursuit of which he will at last weary out and destroy feudal systems, mighty churches, medieval orders, slaveholding oligarchies, and what else may stand in his way. Then he will enlarge his social consciousness from his individual self to the nation of which he is a unit; and he will have his national liberty as he had his personal liberty, nor will all the excellent reasons in the world avail finally against him. . . . The third step is the federation of nationalities; but you cannot induce him to forgo the achieve-

ment of national independence on the ground that inter-
national federation is a step higher.
("A Crib for Home Rulers," 1888)

When Shaw wrote these words, he was thinking not of medieval
France but of contemporary Ireland. Obviously, he considered the
Hundred Years War an object lesson in the futility of England's
trying to impose its rule on another country against its will. In a
defense of the play he sent to the Theatre Guild, Shaw argued that he
would not have written *Saint Joan* if he had not thought it had
immediate relevance in "a world situation in which we see whole
peoples perishing and dragging us towards the abyss which has swal-
lowed them, all for want of any grasp of the political forces that
move civilization." Today, forty years later, America's frequent
blindness to the meaning of nationalist and social revolutions
throughout the world might have struck him as another cogent example of the consequences of an inadequate philosophy of history.

Shaw's ascription to Joan of crypto-Protestant leanings has
aroused even more controversy than his making her a nationalist.
Once again, Shaw was not the first person to set forth such a theory,
though we may safely speculate that he was not familiar with the
obscure German theological study in which it was originally formu-
lated in 1841. J. M. Robertson, who considered this idea of Joan's
Protestantism a typical Shavian *jeu d'esprit,* rejected it as fantastically
absurd. But since he also admits that the Church has had its Protestant dissenters from the first century on, there seems to be little
reason why he should object to the adjective being applied to Joan.
The real point of course is the meaning to be given to the word
"Protestant." If it is restricted to someone who founds or joins a new
church in opposition to the Church of Rome, then obviously Joan
does not qualify. But Shaw freely admits Joan's devoutness and piety
and her failure to challenge the Church on doctrinal grounds and is
careful to point out that he is using the term only to designate someone who reserves the right to place his private judgment above the
authoritative decision of an ecclesiastical court.

Only at one point does it seem to me that Shaw seriously mis-
interprets Joan's career, and this mistake has to do not with her
character, but with her situation. Shaw sees Joan's trial as preemi-
nently a confrontation between a new prophet and the representatives of the status quo. In this respect he endows it with the same

significance for the Middle Ages that the trial of Socrates had for the history of Athens. But this is to miss a salient fact in fifteenth-century French politics—that the Hundred Years War was a French civil war as well as an Anglo-French conflict. Joan's party was opposed by a group of Frenchmen who were pro-English and pro-Burgundian because of their indignation at the Dauphin's complicity in the murder of Duke John the Fearless. To the extent that he belonged to this party, it is impossible to regard Cauchon as an unbiased spokesman for medieval Catholicism. True, there is, on the other hand, no reason to stereotype Cauchon as a villain as Mark Twain does. But his sincerity at the trial was the sincerity of a man who had committed himself to one side in a bitter political quarrel. Though he was punctilious about points of law even to the extent of exasperating Joan's more violent adversaries, his intimidation of witnesses and scribes at her trial reveals his real commitment. In brief, the court at Rouen was not the impartial tribunal the contemporary Council of Basel might conceivably have been.

But if Shaw inadvertently distorts history, the lesson he is trying to teach—that the saint will encounter his strongest, most dangerous opposition from the most high-minded and best-intentioned members of society—is a true and significant one. Even as a misreading of history, it is more nobly generous than the view of Robertson, who simply affirms in his book that justice was denied Joan because the Christian dogma of belief "excludes the conception of justice, once for all." In addition, it is more cogent than the Church's official argument exculpating itself from responsibility for Joan's death—that Cauchon was simply acting illegally in denying Joan's appeal to the Pope. Can the Church be honestly certain as to what the outcome of that appeal would have been? Joan's spirit, as Shaw noted, was as adamant as Hus's or Luther's. Surely his contention that Joan, if asked to deny her visions at Basel, would have stood her ground there just as firmly in the face of any command to recant, ought to give conscientious Catholics pause for thought. If Shaw, in creating his portrait of a fair and disinterested Cauchon, sought to make amends for the "abominable bigotry" of his Irish Protestant boyhood, he nevertheless, by putting the question candidly and without animus, puts it all the more tellingly. As a result, any disinterested observer with a sense of irony will unavoidably feel there is a little too much that is comically self-congratulatory in the Church's decree of canonization.

Saint Joan, which was the occasion for awarding Shaw the Nobel

Prize, did more than any other play to increase his prestige with the general public. Perhaps in reaction to this, some of his most sympathetic admirers have expressed large reservations about it. It is interesting to note the direction this criticism has taken. Where Victorian audiences would have been shocked by the lively irreverence of the play's opening scene, it has been what we may call the fideistic elements of the drama—its edification, its poetry, and its religious purpose—that have called forth the most significant twentieth-century attacks. In addition, formalist critics have objected to the explicit philosophizing and to the epilogue, which they have regarded as gratuitous to a dramatic tragedy. But, before we consider the play in relation to these matters, we may find it illuminating to look briefly at its individual episodes to see what they tell us about Shaw's intentions.

The first scene immediately makes clear Shaw's voluntarist, antirational view of Joan's temperament. Her encounter with the peppery squire, Baudricourt, is a piece of classical farce. As a feudal leader and a physically vigorous male, Baudricourt tries at first to impress his cringing steward with his own strong-mindedness. But when Joan enters, her soft-spoken determination turns aside the blustering soldier's fulminations as easily as the wind might turn the flame at a volcano's mouth. Baudricourt reveals himself as a fundamentally will-less person, Joan as a woman with a will of iron. Her triumph in the contest between them shows the power of will over circumstances and of belief over doubt. Yet Shaw treats these transcendental themes with positive breeziness, deliberately using his flair for humor to shake any conventionally pious or vapidly romantic preconception of the Maid the audience may be entertaining, even to the point of ending with the absurd pseudo-miracle of the eggs.

Baudricourt has spirit but lacks direction. The courtiers at Chinon, by contrast, know what needs to be done, but are paralyzed, despairing, and unable to look beyond their own self-interest. They are all, in this sense, rational utilitarians. The Dauphin has so little force of conviction that he arouses only laughter when, like the squire, he attempts to put his foot down. On the intellectual side, however, by far the most interesting member of the court is the Archbishop. He is the very spirit of skepticism in its most sophisticated and self-conscious form. Shaw is careful to place him historically by pointing out that he belongs, not to Joan's world of medieval faith, but to the coming age of the Renaissance. He is a humanist scholar with so much of the doubter and cynic about him that Anatole France might either have satirized him as a worldly prelate or hailed him as kindred soul. A hollow fraud as a man of religion, he is nevertheless an astute statesman. He knows, for instance, that the faith of the multitude can very easily be sustained by clever stage effects and that the will to believe creates its own evidence. Still, he realizes that the faith that can move mountains is a force to be reckoned with, however silly the signs the mob accepts as pledges of divine favor. We thus watch the recognition scene with double vision, at once caught up in its drama and at the same time endowed with the Archbishop's skeptical detachment, as Joan unscrupulously (even "craftily," as Shaw expresses it) exploits the superstition of the court for her own ends. For all this, we still inevitably thrill when selfishness and cowardice vanish before Joan's convictions. Faith, which appears to the court to have performed a miracle in guiding Joan to the Dauphin, has in all truth performed a greater miracle still in transforming supine men into potential fighters.

When Joan and Dunois meet at the Loire, Shaw suggests that the force that bears Joan onward is, like Shelley's West Wind, the *Zeitgeist* itself. Up to now we have simply seen this power objectified as the human will in dramatic conflict with obstacles in its way. Joan remains largely unconscious of the broader meaning of her mission or has only the most naïve glimpses of its significance. Finally, however, in the tent scene, we have Joan's antifeudal nationalism and her Protestantism explicitly analyzed for us in the colloquy between Warwick and Cauchon. Edmund Wilson has taken exception to this discussion on the grounds that Chekhov would never have written it. But this is to limit unduly the possibilities of drama as a commentary on human existence. Shaw admits in the play's preface the anachronism of the debate; but the function of the intellectual dramatist, he tells us, is to make his figures "more intelligible to themselves than they would be in real life" by revealing the hidden causes and currents that move individuals and nations. In a sense broader than Aristotle's, Shaw insists that drama must be "more philosophical than history."

The philosophical meaning of *Saint Joan* can be grasped only when we look at the play in relation to the conventional idea of tragedy. Here some teasing critical questions inevitably arise. For instance, is Shaw's philosophy of the life force compatible with the idea of tragedy at all? To the extent that tragic drama is a drama of despair, obviously it is not. Schopenhauer's praise of tragedy as the highest form of poetic art because it dramatizes "the surrender not merely of life, but of the very will-to-live," would hardly have recommended tragedy to Shaw. In this regard, then, Shaw is essentially an antitragic dramatist and belongs to the line of writers who have tended to dethrone tragedy from its place of honor among dramatic forms. But it is by no means possible to write Shaw off as a mere maverick on this account. We tend to forget that the critical tradition which is hostile to "pure" tragedy has been quite as persistent and is historically even older than the tradition which has exalted it. Plato, after all, thought tragedy demoralizing because it fostered the emotions of grief and fear instead of courage and a sense of civic responsibility. In our own day Karl Jaspers has warned us in his *Tragedy Is Not Enough* that the cultivation of a tragic sense can lead to a self-exaltation which is really a dangerous form of self-indulgence. And even Hegel, one feels, if he had strictly followed the logic of his own theory, should have placed a drama of reconciliation like the *Oresteia* above a tragedy like *Antigone,* just as he places a tragedy of ideological conflict like *Antigone* above a play of personal misfortune like *Oedipus.*

Shaw attacks what might be called the infidel side of tragedy; he wants to substitute for the tragedy of despair a tragedy of faith with a radically different aesthetic. To this end he makes his play Hegelian, neo-Gothic (or Pre-Raphaelite), and Promethean, and by implication, anti-Aristotelian, anticlassical and anti-Shakespearean. The extent to which this is the case has not been clear to most readers, some of whom have argued that *Saint Joan* rigorously fulfills the canons of classical tragic art. To a degree they have been misled by Shaw's boast in his preface that he is writing classical tragedy, whereas in fact he only intends by the term "classical" to distinguish any serious, critical approach to literature from popular melodrama. If we look deeper we will even find that the play, far from fulfilling, or even simply ignoring, classical canons, is a deliberate repudiation of classicism as it existed in Greek times and was revived by the Renaissance. Moreover, since Aristotle is par excellence the theorist of classical tragedy, it is specifically a negation of the conception of tragedy set forth in the *Poetics.* Shaw makes this clear at the end of the preface when he declares that the theater in its "Aristotelian moments" is purgatorial, by which, through his punning reference to the doctrine of catharsis, he means to imply that audiences are ultimately bored by attempts to achieve perfection of artistic form and can be fully engrossed only by drama which touches their lives and interests at some vital point.

It should not surprise us to find that, just as *Arms and the Man* is a critique of conventional romance, and *The Devil's Disciple* of conventional melodrama, so *Saint Joan* is a critique of traditionally held theories of tragedy. Aristotle, for example, contends that the death on the stage of a "pre-eminently just or virtuous" person can only outrage the sensibilities of an audience, and that a tragic hero must not be a saint, but a man capable of committing a tragic error. Shaw, by contrast, goes out of his way to show that it is Joan's virtues, and not her defects, which bring about her death. This is the whole point of the cathedral scene, which attacks the sentimental idea that "we needs must love the highest when we see it" by showing how Joan's gifts inevitably provoke hostility. Those critics who, looking for Joan's *hamartia,* have ascribed her downfall to her vanity or her lack of prudence have put a false emphasis on minor details Shaw has introduced merely to humanize his heroine. Others have been deceived by the fact that the Archbishop, foreseeing the end of Joan's career, remarks: "The old Greek tragedy is rising among us. It is the chastisement of hubris." But as we have already noted, Shaw conceives of the Archbishop as a man who belongs to a world alien to Joan's, who recognizes as his kin, not the saints, but Aristotle and Pythagoras. His Greco-Renaissance culture makes him wholly antipathetic to Joan. Those commentators who have quoted his words to show that Shaw is writing classical tragedy have simply missed the irony with which Shaw invests his pronouncements. As we have seen, pride is for Shaw a virtue.

The hostility to Renaissance ethics and aesthetics that pervades *Saint Joan* had its origin in one of the deepest-running currents of Victorian culture. Carlyle and Ruskin both attacked the Renaissance as an age which substituted commercial for religious ideals, and economic individualism for a sense of communal welfare. Ruskin went further and denounced it also as an artistic and cultural debacle in which theatricality and rhetorical posturing had replaced realistic observation and sincere expression of feeling in painting and literature. It is from Ruskin that Shaw derived the idea that Shakespeare had drawn no heroes, that is, men with a positive social or religious philosophy. Hence the "void in the Elizabethan drama" he deplores in his preface as the consequence of the pervading infidelism of the

Renaissance. As an antidote to rhetorical neoclassicism in art, Shaw favored a return to what he calls the Gothic style, which, instead of requiring a uniform elevation of sentiment and diction throughout (that is to say, neoclassical decorum), combined imaginative sublimity with homely realism. Thus *Saint Joan,* with its mixture of broad farce and exaltation, is Pre-Raphaelite in style as well as in substance and closer, in its juxtaposition of comedy and saintliness, to the religious drama of the Middle Ages than to anything in Elizabethan or later theatrical literature. Its aesthetic is that of *Modern Painters* and *The Stones of Venice,* purged of Ruskin's conventional evangelical piety and his nature worship.

The theory of tragedy which comes closest to Shaw's is that set forth by Hegel in his *Philosophy of Fine Art.* That is not to say that Shaw in *Saint Joan* consciously attempted to write a Hegelian drama or that he had even read this or any of Hegel's other voluminous writings on tragedy. Rather, the affinity with Hegel springs from what we may call the natural Hegelianism of Shaw's mind. Certainly *Saint Joan* is Hegelian in its treatment of historical processes, dramatizing as it does the evolving forces of nationalism and individualism and the feudal and authoritarian reactions those movements provoke. Hegel and Shaw both agreed that conflicts of this sort were the very substance of drama. Both ruled out personal ambition and the "hazards of crime" as adequate subjects for high tragedy, though many playwrights (including Shakespeare) have sought to make tragedy out of these ingredients. "Abstract evil," Hegel held, anticipating Shaw, "neither possesses truth in itself, nor does it arouse interest." For each of them the only really significant tragic subjects were those collisions between different moral imperatives, both apparently "good," which make mutually contradictory demands. This is why Hegel thought of *Antigone,* with its conflict between family and social duties, as the archetypal tragedy. But Hegel's most succinct and illuminating remarks on tragedy occur, significantly enough, not in a discussion of a stage play, but of a real historical event, the trial of Socrates:

> In genuine tragedy, then, [there] must be powers both alike moral and justifiable, which from this side and from that, come into collision; and such was the fate of Socrates. His fate therefore is not merely personal, and as it were part of the romance of an individual: it is the general fate,

in all its tragedy—the tragedy of Athens, of Greece, which
is therein carried out. Two opposed Rights come forth: the
one breaks itself to pieces against the other: in this way,
both alike suffer loss; while both alike are justified the one
towards the other: not as if this were right, that other
wrong. On the one side is the religious claim, the unconscious moral habit: the other principle, over against it, is
the equally religious claim—the claim of the consciousness, of the reason, creating a world out of itself, the claim
to eat of the tree of the knowledge of good and evil. The
latter remains the common principle of philosophy for all
time to come.

It is a view of tragedy akin to Hegel's Shaw has in mind when
he insists that Joan's trial must not be seen as popular melodrama but
as the confrontation of antagonistic historical forces of broad significance. Shaw's effort to objectify and depersonalize the situation has
led some commentators to argue that he does not in effect even take
sides. Eric Bentley, usually a perspicacious judge of Shaw's intentions, has described him as writing neither an "individualist defense
of Joan" nor a "collectivist defense of social order" but as merely
"depicting the clash." Obviously, if we have a fatal disagreement
between two apparent "goods," the problem does arise as to how we
should interpret the resulting catastrophe. We might, for instance,
merely respond with the same supine awe we feel on contemplating
the *Titanic*'s smashing into the iceberg. Or, looking at the situation
from the vantage of history, we might adopt the "unripe moment"
attitude. This is, in sum, what Hegel does in the case of Socrates.
Hegel thinks the Athenians were right in condemning Socrates for
encouraging disobedience to parents and for setting his own private
daemon above the state religion. He also maintains that they were
right in reversing their verdict and condemning Socrates' judges a
few years later. The Athenians were simply not historically ready to
accept Socrates on the first occasion; later they had caught up with
him, but he had in the meantime to pay for his forwardness.

But is this really Shaw's attitude toward Joan? Hegel's defense of
the Athenians rests on his general premise that the state is an absolute
incapable of wrong, a position Shaw emphatically rejected. Shaw
pointedly declared that a historian who would defend Joan's burning
would defend anything. We must remember that for Shaw, the

archetypal tragedy is not *Antigone,* but *Prometheus.* His aim is not to defend social stupidities but to educate us out of them. The reason he enters so sympathetically into the mentality of the Inquisition is not to exonerate it, but merely to make his point that the most nefarious institutions and their administrators always seem perfectly justified in their own eyes and in the eyes of most onlookers. Then, too, he wants to destroy any smug suppositions we may be nursing in our minds about a bad past and a good present, and to counteract the all but universal human tendency to decry historical bogeys like the Inquisition and to accept their modern counterparts uncritically. Shaw forces us to look at the trial with the eyes of the fifteenth century, not because he thinks the Inquisition was, even in Hegel's conditional sense of the term, "right," but because the fifteenth century regarded its procedures as perfectly respectable and was just as mistakenly comfortable about them as we are about our own law courts.

Most people have failed to grasp Shaw's real outlook simply because he makes the Inquisitor at the trial a mild, scholarly, saintly old man. But apart from the fact that Shaw seems to have modeled his Inquisitor on the historical Torquemada, who had such a temperament, his intention is to warn us that it is just the sweet, saintly old men who make the most dangerous apologists for judicial crimes. Like Britannus in *Caesar and Cleopatra* and Judge Hallam in *Captain Brassbound's Conversion,* the Inquisitor is sincerely convinced of the horrors that would befall society if the office of judge and our system of social punishments were to be abolished. Allowing the Inquisitor to present his case as cogently as possible, Shaw provides him with a consummately skillful rhetoric which is nevertheless shot through and through with Shavian antijudicial irony:

> Mark what I say: the woman who quarrels with her clothes, and puts on the dress of a man, is like the man who throws off his fur gown and dresses like John the Baptist: they are followed, as surely as the night follows the day, by bands of wild women and men *who refuse to wear any clothes at all.* When maids will neither marry nor take regular vows, and men reject marriage and exalt their lusts into divine inspirations, then, as surely as the summer follows the spring, *they begin with polygamy, and end by incest.* Heresy at first seems innocent and even laudable; but it ends in *such a monstrous horror of unnatural wickedness* that the most tender-

hearted among you, if you saw it at work as I have seen it, would clamor against the mercy of the Church in dealing with it. [Italics added.]

The most striking thing about his speech is the way it plays upon the audience's fears, and particularly, in the passages I have italicized, upon their sexual fears, to intimidate them and justify Inquisitorial practices. The Inquisitor is a melodramatist who thinks the human race would run wild if there were no courts to restrain it. Yet so completely has the impression created by the Inquisitor's gentlemanliness numbed men's ability to detect the hysterical premises of his argument that Shaw found it necessary to remind critics of the drama that the man was, in his eyes, "a most infernal old scoundrel."

The Church's official defense of the Inquisition is to be found in the *Catholic Encyclopedia*. There, a brilliantly written article praises the "truly admirable sanctity" of many of the Inquisitorial judges, and adds, "There is absolutely no reason to look on the medieval ecclesiastical judge as intellectually and morally inferior to the modern judge." Shaw, who apparently studied this essay most carefully in preparing his play, would have agreed; the modern judge and the Inquisitor stand side by side in his vision, too, but not as the saviors of civilization. Both justify terrorism out of panic fear. The rhetoric of Shaw's Inquisitor condemning heresy is identical with that of the defenders of our present-day laws on, say, sexual offenses, obscenity, or drug-taking. The notion that such Inquisitorial attitudes are historically obsolete is soon belied by a little experience of modern criminal prosecutions in these areas. The final irony comes from the fact that the arguments Shaw gives the Inquisitor are exactly those used by the nineteenth-century American Quaker historian H. C. Lea in his monumental *History of the Inquisition* to justify the extermination of the Albigensians, whose ultra-asceticism and contempt for marriage could only, in Lea's view, "have probably resulted in lawless concubinage and the destruction of the institution of the family." With certificates of indemnity like this from Protestant writers, the *Catholic Encyclopedia,* which quotes Lea at length, has no difficulty at all in establishing that the Inquisition was a bulwark of popular social virtues.

The Inquisitor (following the *Encyclopedia*) also argues that only the Inquisition stands between the heretic and popular wrath. Shaw disposes of this line of reasoning in his essay on imprisonment: "It is said, and it is to a certain degree true, that if the Government does not lawfully organize and execute popular vengeance, the populace will rise and execute this vengeance lawlessly for itself. The standard defense of the Inquisition is that without it no heretic's life would have been safe" (Preface to Sidney and Beatrice Webb, *English Prisons under Local Government,* 1922). But, Shaw replies crushingly, a government that cannot control a lynch mob cannot rule at all. It is because of the parallels with modern administration of justice that Shaw puts a forensic tour de force into the mouth of the Inquisitor. The latter is a scoundrel not because he is a medieval ecclesiastic, but because of what he shares in common with most modern Protestants and atheists—a conviction that only through censorship, expiatory punishments, and cruel deterrents can the human race be kept from running amok. In the epilogue that closes the play Shaw pointedly makes him transcend his moment in history and speak for *all* judges in "the blindness and bondage of the law."

Shaw not only despises "justice" as the vengeance principle self-righteously parading in a moral disguise; he is particularly opposed to "the crime of imprisonment." Imagining ourselves superior to the age of the stake and the rack, we tolerate the refined torture of incarceration, and indeed accept it unthinkingly as a matter-of-fact routine until with us, as with the Inquisitor, who has become used to seeing girls burned, "habit is everything." When Joan thinks she can escape death by signing a recantation, she sensibly signs it. The anger she shows on discovering that her choice lies not between the fire and freedom, but the fire and prison, matches Shaw's own contempt for a society that cages men and women without thinking twice about it:

> Bread has no sorrow for me, and water no affliction. But to shut me from the light of the sky and the sight of the fields and flowers; to chain my feet so that I can never again ride with the soldiers nor climb the hills; to make me breathe foul damp darkness, and keep me from everything that brings me back to the love of God when your wickedness and foolishness tempt me to hate Him: all this is worse than the furnace in the Bible that was heated seven times. . . . without these things I cannot live, and by your wanting to take them away from me, or from any human

creature, I know that your counsel is of the devil, and that mine is of God.

It is a sign of our times that though literary critics have commented on Joan's diction in this speech, none have pointed out that, as members of a civilization capable of locking men up for fifty or sixty years, we are as guilty as her judges and companion objects of her—and Shaw's—scorn.

This same blindness to the realities of human suffering afflicts De Stogumber, the Joan-baiting English chaplain in Shaw's play. In him, Shaw provides us with a fifteenth-century analogue of the anti-Hun jingoism of World War I and the insane patriotism that prompted the Black and Tan terror in Ireland. What chiefly characterizes the priest's hatred is its abstract, unimaginative quality. When De Stogumber actually witnesses Joan's burning, he reacts hysterically, and his dramatic breakdown provides Shaw's tragedy with its note of pity and terror. But Shaw does not want to purge us of these emotions: his aim is not to produce a catharsis. Instead, he introduces them with the intention of warning us of our own insensitivity to cruelty and of the danger of giving rein to the feelings roused by war panic.

The defeats of Prometheus are the "staple of tragedy," Shaw wrote in a review in the nineties. Joan's life was for him a historical tragedy in the Promethean mold, in which "all the forces that bring about the catastrophe are on the grandest scale; and the individual soul on which they press is of the most indomitable force and temper." Like Prometheus, Joan challenges the gods, and though, like him, she fails, she also resembles the Greek hero in showing a steadfast courage that speaks to the ages. But of course the failure is not the whole story. The defeats of Prometheus, looked at from the perspective of history, have a way of losing their tragic quality and taking on some of the ironic aspects of tragicomedy. That is what Shaw means by declaring in his preface that when we kill saintly prophets, "the angels may weep at the murder, but the gods laugh at the murderers." Eventually the moment of horror gives way to the moment of philosophical bemusement as we observe mankind revering and worshiping what it first feared and loathed.

In the epilogue to *Saint Joan* we hear the laughter of the gods. Shaw's seriocomic postscript tells us of Joan's canonization, but denies us any sentimental glow of pleasure at seeing the golden aureole fitted into place or sense of gratification at the knowledge of justice done. The actors of her drama all praise her, but they also flinch at the idea of her return to life. Warwick, the eternal politician, admits that he would once more have to face political necessities; Cauchon, the eternal priest, can find no way of distinguishing private judgment from diabolical possession; and the Inquisitor is unable to see how the scourge he calls justice could be dispensed with. Only that modest pragmatist Charles VI is able to understand that what ails the leaders of Church and State is simply that they are "not big enough" for Joan. The world will continue to kill its saints and heroes until it has grown to their stature and produced a society of saints and heroes. Nor until we conquer that fear which is ultimately a fear of ourselves will this be possible. In the meantime, any certificate of sanctification we may issue for Joan remains factitious if it does not imply a toleration for future heretics.

Saint Joan is the last of Shaw's major plays. What he wrote after it is by way of postscript to his career as a playwright, a resetting of the themes of his major works in new keys. Such satires as *The Apple Cart, Too True to Be Good,* and *Geneva* show him responding to a new world mood and to new world crises. But delightful and provocative as some of these sunset dramas are, they add nothing essential to our understanding of Shaw as a world dramatist and critic of civilization. *Saint Joan* stands alone as Shaw's last great tribute to human greatness. As such, it is one of the supreme statements of religious faith in a post-Christian world, the final masterpiece of a man who was willing to hope and think and challenge his readers to the end.

The Histories

Margery M. Morgan

Brecht, and later Weiss, made of the Shavian history play one of the most powerful conventions of modern drama. If only on this account, it is worth going back to discover more precisely the nature of Shaw's achievement in the mode. He was certainly attracted to the historical play: *The Man of Destiny, The Devil's Disciple, Caesar and Cleopatra, Androcles and the Lion, The Dark Lady of the Sonnets, Saint Joan, In Good King Charles's Golden Days,* and the more trifling *Great Catherine* and *The Six of Calais* represent all phases of his long career and fall into the same general category, "historical." Even *Geneva* is subtitled "A Fancied Page of History," a variant on the description applied to *Good King Charles:* "A True History that Never Happened." Of course, all classic drama, when not performed in modern dress, takes on a certain historical colouring, and Shaw was not averse to giving some of his plays the patina of Old Masters. Traditional styles are part of the medium of artistic communication. Shaw entered the theatre at a time when the high styles of Ibsenite realism, in modern dress, and Greek ritualism were challenging the monopoly of Shakespearian tradition, the latest stronghold of which was Irving's theatre. Not even the strongest of orthodoxies was ruled out of bounds in Shaw's idiosyncratic experimentation with the range of conventions open to him, "high" and popular. Historical drama is a principal form of costume drama, and Shaw practised it as he practised other varieties, including the Ruritanian romance.

From *The Shavian Playground: An Exploration of the Art of George Bernard Shaw.* © 1972 by Margery M. Morgan. Methuen, 1972.

Whatever the precise dramatic content, costume is part of the pleasurable make-believe which is the strong, central appeal of theatre.

"All dress is fancy dress, is it not, except our natural skins?" says Dunois, and the epilogue to *Saint Joan* graphically establishes a relativism whereby everything distinctive of period, even the top-hatted uniform of twentieth-century man, shows up as the equipment of human play, or dilettante experiment. Neither Shaw, nor Brecht following him, is concerned with historical perspective, with the past as distant and profoundly different from the present. The sense of genuine cultural otherness affecting ways of thought or even the constitution of the mind in remote periods is minimized by both dramatists. However ancient a fashion the costumes represent, the consciousness of the wearers is modern: they talk anachronistically, as with foreknowledge of modern issues. Famous names are attached to characters whose essence is the familiar, the ordinary. Such "historical" drama is merely a special area of fantasy.

The relation between the romantic melodrama and the historical material in *The Devil's Disciple* is not close and precise. The choice of setting is exploited only in a very general way: the rebellion of the American colonies provides a political analogy to Dick Dudgeon's antireligion; and the period is also aptly chosen in that Dick's creed is a version of the challenge Blake actually issued to the religious orthodoxies of the time. More substantially the play records the dramatist's imaginative progress from the strong attraction of a romantic rebel pose (Dick Dudgeon) to an antithetical attitude of cheerful, energetic, and aggressive practicality (Anthony Anderson). The shift is from a mood of doomed defiance to one intent on victory. But it involves trying out the poses on an audience: first on the naïve Effie, who registers the emotional appeal of the more Byronic figure, then on the more sophisticated Judith who, as surrogate of a sentimentally inclined public, is confounded and exposed twice over with a gratuitousness reminiscent of the treatment of Marian in *The Irrational Knot*. Judith's idealization of both men offers two versions of the hero-according-to-woman's-morality that Shaw ultimately rejects for the hero coolly acknowledged by the detached and rational male observer (General Burgoyne, himself too deficient in human warmth for heroic stature). Shaw was certainly at this stage concerned to discover a heroic image, and the conventions of historical drama kept him in countenance. The values the play asserts are the same as he put forward in nonhistorical drama: authentic and generous feeling, as opposed both to coldness (here the negative coldness of Mrs Dudgeon and the inhumanity of Burgoyne) and to false sentiment, is celebrated as in *You Never Can Tell;* the rejection of self-sacrifice and idealized failure for self-fulfilment and success was to be much more forcefully presented in *Major Barbara.*

A comment in the preface to the much later *Good King Charles* represents an occasional Shavian claim that the history in his plays has a more serious, scientific value: "The 'histories' of Shakespear are chronicles dramatized; and my own chief historical plays, Caesar and Cleopatra and St. Joan, are fully documented chronicle plays of this type. Familiarity with them would get a student safely through examination papers on their periods." Apart from the characteristic scornful aside on formal education, this indicates the rules of the game which Shaw, perhaps only subconsciously, recognized as necessary disciplines to such an imagination as his. His normal preference for fantasy has its negative aspect: it exonerates him from the precision that contemporary realism must exact if it is not to be merely unconvincing and inept. Another kind of precision is needed to give shape and weight to what otherwise might be no more than the whimsies of an idle mind. Whether the given facts were true or not, working strictly within their terms was an aid to concentration. In *Caesar and Cleopatra,* for instance, history as every schoolboy knew it in Macaulay's day is the basis of the episodes chosen for representation on stage and the matter of extra-scenic allusion. Caesar as Latin author, recalling the Gallic wars, was only too well known in the classroom and now made more congenial in an actor's impersonation that dodges the pedant to appeal directly to his pupils. The references back to the death of Pompey and forward to the assassination on the Ides of March and the story of Cleopatra and Mark Antony are among the odds-and-ends of universal education that stick in most minds. The business of Cleopatra hiding in the carpet, a picturesque anecdote that Shakespeare found in Plutarch, like the "miracles" of Joan's identification of the Dauphin or the changing of the wind before Orleans, is typical of legendary history, an aspect of folk tradition tenaciously defiant of scientific questioning. Even in *Saint Joan,* Shaw was less inclined to verify what his authorities reported than to take over the material they offered and base his new synoptic version of the story upon it. He justified his

treatment of the characters by claiming that it was not inconsistent
with the available documentary evidence; but that is a late instance of
the Platonic confusion over truth and fiction, over art as an imitation
of life. The play stands as a self-consistent fable, simply meaningful
in a way that life, and history as a record of life, cannot be.

The association with folk education is crucial. In these plays,
Shaw proceeds like a village schoolmaster, inspired with a didactic
purpose that outruns his expert knowledge. He gets on to the stage,
in *Caesar and Cleopatra,* a model of the Sphinx (little enough for the
theatre), the Palace of Alexandria and its roof-garden, the Pharos and
its lighthouse, a working model of an ancient Egyptian steam-
powered crane, Cleopatra's miniature shrine of the Nile and, in the
1912 prologue, the Temple of Ra at Memphis; and another Wonder
of the Ancient World, the Alexandrian Library, flares just offstage in
its destruction by fire. It would all be appropriate to the painless
instruction of little Ptolemy. Indeed Caesar, who proves to be a
kindly and playful mentor to children, is an embodiment of the
author's design upon his audiences. The action of the play traces
Caesar's attempt to teach the adolescent Cleopatra to be a queen and,
though the lesson may be all but lost upon her, it is not lost upon us.
His pupil's wayward and impatient attitude to the greater task is
summarily reflected in her demand to play the harp (in one of the
scenes allusively related to episodes in Shakespeare's *Antony and
Cleopatra*):

> CLEOPATRA. . . . you shall teach me. How long will it take?
> MUSICIAN. Not very long: only four years. Your Majesty
> must first become proficient in the philosophy of
> Pythagoras.
> CLEOPATRA. Has she (*indicating the slave*) become proficient
> in the philosophy of Pythagoras?
> MUSICIAN. Oh, she is but a slave. She learns as a dog learns.
> CLEOPATRA. Well, then, I will learn as a dog learns . . . You
> shall give me a lesson every day for a fortnight . . .
> After that, whenever I strike a false note you shall be
> flogged.

As we shall see, it is probable that Cleopatra's rejection of "the
philosophy of Pythagoras" was more than a joke: it is a sign of her
imprisonment in a decadent civilization from which Caesar tries in

vain to rescue her; he is defeated by her egocentricity, a petty manifestation of the general geocentricity of the Ptolemaic universe.

In effect, Caesar came too late. Mommsen's neglect of Caesarion, the legendary child of Caesar and Cleopatra and his misleading reference to a sixteen-year-old Cleopatra—she seems to have been twenty when Caesar was in Egypt—served Shaw's purposes well. As the inclusion of her little brother in the play shows up, Cleopatra has lost the uncorrupt innocence of the child, though she has not yet attained the self-possession—far less the wisdom—of maturity. The notions of greatness that Caesar rejects befit her adolescence. But her nubile fascination is already strong, calculated to affect audiences as it affects Caesar himself. So the dangerousness, even viciousness, of romantic pretensions in politics and the closeness of tyranny and cruelty to notions of honour are associated with the image of a budding *femme fatale*. At last the monstrous femininity growing in Cleopatra is fully revealed to recognition: separately embodied in the savage and dominating black slave, Ftatateeta, stupid, bloated and drunk on blood. (Only when Cleopatra has taken Ftatateeta's values to herself does the Nurse act as a true slave and not the power behind the throne that she was at the start of the play.)

The peculiar modification Shaw's attitude to women gives to his lesson-plays was not taken over by Brecht. Andrea, who is a child when Galileo first undertakes to explain to him the scientific principles at issue in terms as plain and simple as possible, aided by a demonstration that is a game in itself, remains a touchstone of virtue to the end of *Galileo Galilei;* and the Little Monk is another innocent. The simplicity of the peasant heroine Grusha and the folk naïveté of the basic fable of *The Caucasian Chalk Circle* (even Azdak is a picaresque figure familiar enough in a certain type of folktale) match the quality of receptivity the Singer presumes in his audience—on stage in the prologue and in the auditorium. In this respect, at least, Shaw's relation to his audience seems more complex if not more sophisticated. And, if we look forward and compare Brecht's down-to-earth, yet radiant, Grusha with Shaw's plain peasant lass from Domrémy, it is very evident that the latter is no embodiment of instinctive virtue: Grusha's maternal benevolence has to be complemented by the wiliness of Azdak for she, like Joan, has insufficient saving guile; but Joan represents herself as not maternal at all (her liking to play with children is a soldier's characteristic) and her virtue, far from being rooted in her female nature, is identified rather with her revolt against that nature. All told, the differences seem related to Shaw's more complete enclosure within a middle-class society and its ways of thinking and feeling.

There is a sense in which historical colouring is meaningful to both Shaw and Brecht, and not just as part of the carnival. Both had derived from Marx a sense of the value of history, of the coherent interpretation of the past as a political determinant, and they are concerned in their plays with the relation between men's views of the universe, including the retrospective view, and their behaviour in the present. Not fact, but belief, is crucial. The form Shaw's interpretation of history takes is more generally Hegelian than precisely Marxist. He presents historical process as incarnated in the career of great human beings, whose greatness is identifiable with the way in which they are forerunners of a new era and its emergent values. Thus both Caesar and Joan are drawn as Messiah figures, Caesar anticipating Christ and Joan (like the nonhistorical Barbara) reenacting the mission, challenge, and Passion of Christ. The perspective embraces the modern world. Thus Caesar announces a New Law in opposition to the Old Law of vengeance:

> If one man in all the world can be found, now or forever, to know that you did wrong, that man will have either to conquer the world as I have, or be crucified by it. . . . And so, to the end of history, murder shall breed murder, always in the name of right and honor and peace, until the gods are tired of blood and create a race that can understand.

The fallacy of the popular nineteenth-century belief in progress and the mistaken notion that humanity has learnt through experience *in* history are rejected here, as they are tacitly rejected in Shaw's general artistic annihilation of historical difference. The movement of change appears to be cyclic, the same challenge confronting men as individuals in succeeding generations.

Indeed history in Shaw's plays, as in Brecht's and Weiss's, is a moral fable for the dramatist's contemporaries, and it is not too surprising to find the issues of *Saint Joan* raised by Shaw in that earlier disquisitory play with twentieth-century characters, *Getting Married*. The Bishop, his Chaplain, and the young man-about-town, Sinjon Hotchkiss, have witnessed a manifestation of Mrs George's clairvoyant powers:

SOAMES. My lord: is this possession by the devil?

THE BISHOP. Or the ecstasy of a saint?

HOTCHKISS. Or the convulsion of the pythoness on the
tripod?

SOAMES. Shall we take you and burn you?

THE BISHOP. Or take you and canonize you?

HOTCHKISS (*gaily*). Or take you as a matter of course?

The questions are applicable to any highly individualized human
being whose challenge to the social order is fundamentally a matter
of superior personal quality. The phenomenon of "personal gravity," with which such late plays as *The Apple Cart* and *The
Millionairess* are explicitly concerned, is here seen in another aspect:
the most highly evolved, most naturally gifted person becomes leader
in any society—unless the mob turns on him. The conflict is always
between the great man and mass-consciousness, between individual
moral responsibility and undifferentiated force.

The solution Hotchkiss proposes comes in the tone of the comic
dramatist whose historical "realism" means in practice the rejection
of epic glorification, nobility of sentiment, and dignity of style in
favour of a drama of tantrums and sulks, domestic images, and
farcical incident. The Shavian Caesar is Bluntschli in a toga; his Joan
has characteristics of the pantomime Principal Boy; the extreme is
reached in such playlets as *Great Catherine* and *The Six of Calais,*
whose Punch-and-Judy humours give opportunity for histrionic
barnstorming at the opposite pole from subtle psychological realism.
Shaw's reaction to conventional heroic figures is certainly ambivalent: they fascinate his imagination, yet prompt him to expose the
ridiculousness of the human being and, in particular, the childishness
in the man. In his version of Hegelianism, the great individual is
redefined as ordinary foolish man extraordinarily endowed (viz.
Napoleon) or just extraordinarily free of cant, pretentiousness, and
self-delusion: Charles II without his wig or, alternatively, the distinguished company he meets: "Here is Pastor Fox, a king in his
meeting house. . . . Here is Mr Newton, a king in the new Royal
Society. Here is Godfrey Kneller: a king among painters. I can make
you duchesses and your sons dukes; but who would be mere dukes
or duchesses if they could be kings and queens?"

The later plays, especially, are addicted to astronomical images
of change—not gradual, but sudden and cataclysmic: the collison of

stars in *The Apple Cart;* the orbit of the Earth leaping to its next quantum at the end of *Geneva;* in *Good King Charles* a backward view of the shift from a Ptolemaic to a Copernican universe and premonitions of the abandonment of Newtonian physics with the discoveries of Einstein. Galileo is Newton's hero, whom he defends against the ignorant arrogance of James, Duke of York; the period of *Saint Joan* (as of *Caesar and Cleopatra*) is too early for an anticipation of Galileo, and so the playwright there associates a new cosmology with rediscovery of neglected ancient truth:

> THE ARCHBISHOP. . . . There is a new spirit rising in men: we are at the dawning of a wider epoch. If I were a simple monk, and had not to rule men, I should seek peace for my spirit with Aristotle and Pythagoras rather than with the saints and their miracles.

And Pythagoras is then identified as "A sage who held that the earth is round, and that it moves round the sun." Brecht's Galileo is less of a professional politician than Shaw's Archbishop, but what he sees through his telescope teaches him a political lesson that he passes on to his friend, the little Monk, and "it's nothing to do with the planets, it's to do with the peasants in the Campagna." The death of old piety is a signal for the release of men: "The heavens are empty, and there is a gale of laughter over that." The scientific nature of the cosmic imagery is not merely fortuitous: human society may demonstrate the same evolutionary principle as is at work in the rest of nature. But a total altering of the cosmic view has revolutionary implications.

The shift from one historical cycle to another is consistently associated by Shaw with the abandonment of an outworn faith. Caesar, who chooses to leave the great library burning in order to make for the lighthouse, is more successful than George Fox (in *Good King Charles*) in rooting out "the sin of idolatry." When the Romans triumph, the Egyptian priests offer their images for sale at bargain prices, and "Apis the all-knowing" goes for five talents. Part of the strength of a Roman legion is that it is, as Bel Affris says in the original prologue, like a man with no religion. But religion as the Egyptians understand it, and as it is demonstrated in the rites Cleopatra celebrates, is superstition wedded to barbarism; Caesar's common sense, humility, and infinite readiness to forgive his enemies are premonitions of the virtues of Christ. What happens in the heavens, in Shavian drama, shows the hand of God that can shatter all orthodoxies. The "splendid drumming in the sky," at the end of *Heartbreak House,* is as miraculous as the moments out of time when the clock of the universe stopped, or was turned back, which Newton, Fox, and Charles consider together: moments of the "sun which stood still upon Gibeon and the moon in the Valley of Ajalon" (an appropriately biblical image which Tennyson had used in "Locksley Hall," along with the "cycle of Cathay," to denote a rejection of the post-Darwinian ideal of progress), or when "the shadow on the dial of Ahaz went ten degrees backward as a sign from God." The analogy of Paley's watch ceases to be inexorably determinist when it is extended by implication in this way.

Caesar and Cleopatra is a notable early instance of Shaw's preference of a loose construction to an organically developed plot. He admitted that act 3 might be dispensed with in performance to cut down playing time. Yet the act justifies its presence as a celebration of the moment of creative freedom in the midst of events. It is recognizable as an upgraded harlequinade: the date-eating episode and the clowning with Britannus, the butt, usher in a version of the pantomime chase. The absurdity of Cleopatra hidden in the carpet blends with the relief from tedious thought and feeling that the acrobatics represent, with the general panache of Apollodorus, the music of the barcarole he sings, and the fancy-free sentiment it conveys. The evocation of sunlit air and sea and the imagery of flight are matched by the buoyancy of Caesar's own mood as he dives into the sea after Apollodorus (there is, after all, a way out for men bold enough to take it). As he swims with Cleopatra on his back, he is transformed into a dolphin; and, as Shaw filched the image from Shakespeare's Antony, one wonders if he was aware of its traditional use as a Christ-symbol, silently apt in the present context.

The physical energy of this act throws into relief the static quality of much of the play, when Caesar sits twiddling his thumbs and talking, and the audience is as disappointed as Cleopatra of decisive action. (Act 2 is a model of indecisive action, checked and reversed.) Indeed it is only in act 4, when Cleopatra seizes the initiative and, by her actions, swings the play close to a tragic catastrophe that a strong dramatic rhythm emerges. It lapses again when chance and the timing of events bring up the reinforcements to save the situation that had seemingly outrun Caesar's power of saving it. To resist tragedy appears to have been Shaw's fundamental intention and his most deliberate departure from Shakespearian example. He was willing to indulge the late nineteenth-century taste for scene painting and exploit the glamour of stage lighting, particularly in acts 1 and 4; these could be turned to good account as illusionary aids to Cleopatra's histrionic aping of an authority that is not in her character. Extending the play to Rome and the Ides of March would have been to involve his hero in what he himself would judge a romantic sham. "I do not make human sacrifices to my honor," declares Caesar; it is exactly what Cleopatra does, and it doesn't show up as honourable. There is no moral pretentiousness about Rufio's "natural" slaying of the savage beast, as there is about "honour" and "revenge" and, all but inevitably, about tragedy and tragic heroism, too.

Caesar balances not thinking too well of human nature by not thinking too badly of it either; the method is close enough to Hotchkiss's notion of taking it "as a matter of course." The genius of comedy stays close to Caesar in the person of Apollodorus, amateur of the aesthetic (not theatrical), who contributes to the play a gaiety like that of *You Never Can Tell*. Philip's jesting reference to Valentine as "the man of ivory and gold," would be apt to Apollodorus, through whom the nature of Phoebus Apollo surely shines. Nothing can go finally and irrevocably wrong in a world that he inhabits. (Cleopatra, masquerading as pigeons' eggs, smothering in a carpet, is not only ludicrous, but stuffy, beside his grace). But the play is composed largely on a principle of contrasted tones, and Lucius Septimius is a dark counterpart to Apollodorus's brightness. Gloom-ridden and sinister, the brief appearances of Lucius are ominous of the murder of Pothinus and the slaying of Ftatateeta on the altar, ominous of the treachery and cruelty of Cleopatra, at the same time as they recall the old sins and political mistakes of the historical Caesar. Lucius Septimius can be regarded as a dark shadow cast by Shakespeare's baleful Caesar, focus of the superstition which Shaw has transferred to the Egyptians. He is redeemed by the clemency of the Shavian Caesar who does not idealize evil; and so the darkness is dispersed at the end of the play, except for the knowledge that the Ides of March lie ahead: the victory of reason is not absolute.

Saint Joan invokes the concept of tragedy more decisively, but still repudiates it. It does so by virtue of being a passion play even more than by being—sporadically—a pantomime. The episodic structure itself recalls the pageant-drama, and the successive examinations of Joan are roughly analogous to the bringing of Christ before Annas, Caiaphas, and Pilate in the orthodox Christian passion play. Shaw's insistence on the fairness of her judges brings them collectively close to the attitude of Pilate, and the wary collaboration of the Inquisition with English feudal power reproduces in a very general way the conditions of collaboration between Jewish orthodoxy and the Roman Imperium that led to the trial and execution of Christ. Shaw's wish to assimilate the story of Joan to that of Christ is confirmed in a series of parallels too insistent to be casual. Warwick's proposal, in scene 4, to "buy" Joan is followed up, just before the scene ends, by De Stogumber's echo of Caiaphas: "It is expedient that one woman die for the people." The symbolic figure of Judas is remembered in Joan's reproof to the Dauphin, "Wilt be a poor little Judas, and betray me and Him that sent me?" (scene 2), and, after her burning, in De Stogumber's verdict on himself, "I am no better than Judas: I will hang myself." He comments on the crowd at the execution, "Some of the people laughed at her. They would have laughed at Christ," and he unconsciously aligns himself with those for whom the Christian Saviour died on the Cross: "I did not know what I was doing." Joan's naïve vision of herself as a Messiah not only reveals the blend of simplicity and self-confident pride in her own character, it prompts fresh recognition of the breathtaking arrogance of Christ's claims by removing them from a context of pious acceptance and exposing them to a more sceptical consideration (a necessary part of the attempt to turn religion back into history). Her message to Baudricourt, in scene 1, is uncompromising: "It is the will of God that you are to do what He has put into my mind." The effect of her unconscious echoing of Christ's words, as in her challenge to the Dauphin "Art for or against me?" may be doubly ironic. For the device helps to establish her as a Christ-surrogate in the play but also enables us to see the closeness of her piety to blasphemy and the megalomaniac quality not only in *her* self-devotion but inseparable from the humanity of the Saviour. The impression given may be incidentally comic: "I do know better than any of you seem to. And . . . I never speak unless I know I am right." Cauchon's judgement of such self-assurance—"She acts as if she herself were the Church"—brings out an analogy with Christ's proposal of a New Law to supersede the Old Law and makes it possible for the detached mind to see a humorous aspect in that too. The brash irreverence of Shaw's juvenile passion play is avoided by the indirection of his approach here; but the basic attitude of mind is not so different; he was concerned to naturalize more than the sanctity of Joan and *her* miracles. ("A miracle," explains the Archbishop with the familiarity of professionalism, "is an event which creates faith.")

The addition of the epilogue most effectively debars an interpretation of the play simply as a study of Joan's self-delusion and the imaginative compulsion it exerts over others. Her final cry at the trial, "I am His child, and you are not fit that I should live among you," sounds a maddened defiance without any comic overtones. The note of feeling is apt to the approach of death in torment; it also signals the translation of the human being into a world of the spirit. And, for all its extravaganza form, the epilogue serves as Shaw's instrument to extend the story of Joan beyond the apparent finality of her death at the stake to a resurrection and ascension. Indeed his conformation of her legend to the central myth and ritual of Christianity is made remarkably complete, though the manner of it is condensed and allusive. The Harrowing of Hell is intimated in the liberation of the Soldier for his day's parole in the calendar of saints. The presentation of De Stogumber as a man without imagination, who needs to see with his bodily eyes before he can believe, recalls the incredulity and conversion of Thomas. The décor of the Dauphin's bedchamber, with its candles and painted tapestries in which *"the prevailing yellow and red . . . is somewhat flamelike when the folds breathe in the wind"* is an appropriate background to a dream vision of Joan, as it suggests the *auto-da-fé* which was not actually presented on stage; taken in conjunction with the wind that now and again rushes through the chamber, it can hint an imaginative fusion of the appearance of the crucified Saviour in the midst of his disciples gathered in an upper room with the scene of Pentecost, the coming of the Holy Ghost in tongues of flame, and a rushing mighty wind. Gospel gives way to liturgy, with a formal adaptation of the *Te Deum,* addressed to the newly canonized Joan:

> The girls in the field praise thee . . .
> The dying soldiers praise thee . . .
> The cunning counsellors praise thee . . .
> The foolish old men on their deathbeds praise thee . . .
> The judges in the blindness and bondage of the law
> > praise thee, etc.

Her response "Woe unto me when all men praise me!" slightly adapts an uncompleted quotation. The full text (Luke 6:26) is surely significant for an understanding of Shaw's intention over the whole play, whether or not he expected his audiences to complete it in their minds: "Woe unto you, when all men shall speak well of you! *for so did their fathers to the false prophets*" (my italics).

Cauchon's last words in the epilogue, "mortal eyes cannot distinguish the saint from the heretic," express the moral of the play. From his Archimedean point, equidistant from the historical past and the twentieth century, Shaw poses the question of whether Joan was wrong, whether her private judgement brought good or evil to the world. The difficulty has presented itself to the heroine herself at her trial in subjective terms: "What other judgement can I judge by but my own?" Only a dialectical or dramatic mode can contain the dangerousness of that truth. It will not solve the problem to see the churchmen giving an entirely spurious authority to their private judgements by identifying them with the institution of the Church, for Joan surpasses them in identifying hers with the will of God and the messages of the saints.

She is, of course, innocent in the sense that the Inquisitor recognizes, innocent through her uncorrupted instincts: she is not self-seeking; she has a natural friendliness to all; her intentions are good. Yet De Stogumber could be speaking for her in his words, "I did not know what I was doing." Such childish innocence is dangerous in a world of power. The play was completed and performed in 1923 when the historical process Shaw (through Warwick and Cauchon) represents Joan as initiating had reached its evolutionary climax. Cauchon's prophecies must then have had the ring of topical comment: "The Catholic Church knows only one realm, and that is the realm of Christ's kingdom. Divide that kingdom into nations, and you dethrone Christ. Dethrone Christ, and who will stand between our throats and the sword? The world will perish in a welter of war." This is not simply the voice of the medieval Church; the intellectual attitude which saw the high medieval period as the end of a cycle of faith and civilization giving way to the barbarism of the modern world was currently respectable just before and after the First World War. Yeats looked back to the beginning of the Christian cycle itself for a parallel to the contemporary situation:

> Odour of blood when Christ was slain
> Made all Platonic tolerance vain
> And vain all Doric discipline;

and his anticipations were symbolized in the "rough beast" of the Second Coming. As for Joan, Shaw's new Christ of the fifteenth century, she stands to Cauchon as a figure of similar dark prognostication: "It will be a world of blood, of fury, of devastation, of each man striving for his own hand: in the end a world wrecked back into barbarism."

An interpretation of Joan as innocent fool is carried to some extent by the pantomime conventions introduced into the play and reasserted in the epilogue after lapsing in the trial scene. The theatrical unreality of pantomime also serves to keep her in focus as an enigma challenging the mind, never quite a tragic heroine or a victim whose boldness is finally pathetic. The first scene, with its blustering baron and hens that won't lay, the nicknames, Polly and Jack and Dick the Archer, which the peasant lass impertinently applies to Baudricourt's men, the comic abuse ("The worst, most incompetent, drivelling snivelling jibbering jabbering idiot of a steward in France"), the cool high-handedness of the girl with her feudal lord ("I have arranged it all: you have only to give the order") establish the relation to Christmas pantomime quite firmly before the final absurd "miracle"—"The hens are laying like mad, sir. Five dozen eggs!"—sets its seal on the style. Appropriately, Bluebeard himself takes the stage in the second scene, though admittedly it is Bluebeard closer to actuality and remoter from fairy tale than usual, in a poise that the whole scene reflects. Joan appears here in the usual masculine garb of the Principal Boy for the first time, and the extent to which Shaw's characterization of her is a refinement on the type of Jack or Dick (who grows up to play Widow Twankey) is the more evident: her self-confidence, her humour, her easy friendliness with all ranks, her brave attitudes, and her bossiness are rooted in the convention; and the language she speaks ("Coom, Bluebeard! Thou canst not fool me. Where be Dauphin?") is native to no other area. The Dauphin's clowning supplies her with congenial company. For a moment their shared response to the appearance and manners of the Duchess de la Trémouille can delude us into seeing this only other female role in the play as another female impersonation—an "ugly sister," perhaps:

> THE DUCHESS (*coldly*). Will you allow me to pass, please?
> JOAN (*hastily rising, and standing back*). Beg pardon, ma'am,
>   I am sure.

> *The Duchess passes on. Joan stares after her; then whispers to the Dauphin.*
>
> JOAN. Be that Queen?
>
> CHARLES. No. She thinks she is.
>
> JOAN (*again staring after the Duchess*). Oo-oo-ooh! (*Her awe-struck amazement at the figure cut by the magnificently dressed lady is not wholly complimentary.*)

The epithet for la Trémouille himself follows pat, with no shift of style: "Who be old Gruff-and-Grum?"

Though he never ceases to cut capers, the Dauphin merely *plays* the fool, while being as astute as any character in the drama. Even in scene 2, his shrewdness penetrates further into the complexities of an offstage world than pantomime can usually allow: "I can tell you that one good treaty is worth ten good fights. These fighting fellows lose all on the treaties that they gain on the fights" (this had a topical edge after Versailles, of course). His coolly pragmatic viewpoint under-cuts Joan's ectasies even in the epilogue: "You people with your heads in the sky spend all your time trying to turn the world upside down." History played into Shaw's hands by letting the dogs of comedy, Charles and Dunois (who also views Joan soberly and never sees her other than life-size—as Hotchkiss proposes taking Mrs George for granted), survive and prosper through the period of the epilogue. It also conveniently debarred Charles from the trial scene and the preparations for it, when the sense of make-believe had to be suspended for the intensity of crisis to be complete, and the impres-sion of Joan as a real human being required a playing down of the stage type. Yet these scenes substitute another clown for the Dau-phin: the Chaplain to Warwick, De Stogumber, whose absurdity modulates readily into pathos.

Though politically they are on opposite sides, there is a percep-tible similarity between De Stogumber and Joan. Both are innocents, country folk, and patriots, out of their depth among men of subtler, more sophisticated mind. But the Chaplain is a representative of the common man, and Joan of the extraordinary, "original" human be-ing; the fault he exposes is lack of imaginative understanding, whereas she plays into her judges' hands through the power of her imagina-tion, the fact that she thinks in images. Apart from this, his com-monplace ignorance, prejudice, and self-righteousness, the narrow bigotry of his nationalism and anti-Catholicism, caricature the attitudes of her more heroic personality at the same time as they make him a figure of the crude English philistinism which was Shaw's perpetual Aunt Sally. By balancing the two simpletons in his design, Shaw effectively throws into relief the questionableness of the principles Joan represents. "Sancta simplicitas!" is the blessing Cauchon confers upon De Stogumber's folly and the cruelty it embraces. Her friend, the Dauphin, is less able to contain his impatience with Joan's self-justified fanaticism, the awkward and obstinate aspect of original genius: "It always comes back to the same thing. She is right; and everyone else is wrong."

Charles and Dunois do more than the other characters in the play to keep Joan a natural size and unfalsified by glamour. (It may be worth remarking that, in general type, Charles is a more stylized version of the Shavian Caesar and Dunois a less flamboyant, more mature Apollodorus.) Dunois, in particular, responds to her with a liking that never disturbs his judgement or his sense of professional superiority. He has no doubt about how much of the credit is due to Joan, how much to himself, and no doubt that, when she is captured, he can do without her: "Yes: I shall drive them out. . . . I have learnt my lesson, and taken their measure. . . . I have beaten them before; and I shall beat them again." His freedom from infatuation enables him to foretell her fate on reasonable grounds, and there is a Cromwellian balance that she notably lacks in his hard, practical sense, untainted by any superstition: "I tell you as a soldier that God is no man's daily drudge, and no maid's either . . . once on your feet you must fight with all your might and all your craft." He is as brutal as Undershaft in his verdict on mere idealism: "Some day she will go ahead when she has only ten men to do the work of a hundred. And then she will find that God is on the side of the big battalions." Under so clear and realistic a gaze, Joan's complaint that "the world is too wicked for me" sounds less like pride of spiritual perfection than a sigh of naïve despair that the world is not simple.

In the epilogue, the *revenante* Joan can be allowed a more sophisticated understanding of things. Her raillery of Cauchon (who is the tragic figure of the epilogue)—"Still dreaming of justice, Peter? See what justice came to with me!"—is not so much glibly satiric of the ways of the public world as lucidly perceptive of the truth to which this play with its trial scene testifies as absolutely as *The Doctor's Dilemma* did in its lighter vein: that justice, if it is more than a game, is an ideal which it is not desirable to have translated into actual terms. The dramatic verdict of *Saint Joan,* too, goes against justice in favour of irony: the ability to perceive and weigh all the issues and, if choice is compelled, to preserve a knowledge of its provisional and limited validity. Such irony recognizes what is admirable in the heroic nature, but won't follow it to hell. So Charles adds his share to the *Te Deum:* "The unpretending praise thee, because thou hast taken upon thyself the heroic burdens that are too heavy for them."

Yet it is part of the expansive ironic vision that it should know its own weakness: its very lack of the direct simplicity, the absolute commitment, which is the virtue of the saint and apart from which the cynical Warwicks possess the world. For all Shaw's conscious ingenuity in structuring the play, *Saint Joan* has often been found less than satisfactory by critics, mechanical, facile, or puerile in its incidental effects; yet the central character transcends the play as an imaginative creation. Whereas the writing of the play was not a protracted business, the figure of Joan had long been growing in the dramatist's consciousness as an image of his profoundest dream.

Actresses who either overplay the erotic attractiveness of Joan or suppress it altogether fail in the role. For Shaw's view fluctuates and, though it is faint and subtle and shouldn't protrude on consciousness at all, the feminine erotic quality faintly colours the figure. (It may be worth comparing Shakespeare's Viola who, like Joan, appears in woman's clothing only briefly at the beginning of the play—and was, of course, a more thoroughly androgynous figure in Shakespeare's theatre than in the theatre of Shaw's day.) The kind of appeal this has for audiences and readers recalls the appeal of Dick Dudgeon, in *The Devil's Disciple,* where Shaw utilized the glamour of one type of romantic hero as a vehicle for the serious revision of values. Joan's charm depends on her equal rejection of the Victorian womanly ideal and the identity of fashionable, elegant woman-of-the-world type, or *femme fatale* as it appears to others than men-of-the-world, as Victorian popular instinct had rejected them in its cult of the Principal Boy, more vulgar, even sexually more vital and less insipid than the romantic heroine of pantomime. Joan contains too much that is redolent of the popular stage and indicative of the sturdy peasant for the neurotic associations of the New Woman to corrode her image, though play and preface accept the likelihood that the historical soldier-girl's mission was fired to some extent by abnormal sexuality.

The relevance of the Court's questions about her male attire is endorsed by Joan's own reference to the breach-of-promise case ("I never promised him. I am a soldier: I do not want to be thought of as a woman. I will not dress as a woman"), by her assertion that she has only a soldier's responsiveness to children, and with strongest emphasis from the inventive dramatist himself, by her summing up in the epilogue, that if she *had* been a man, "I should not have bothered you all so much then." Shaw was not intent on a realistic psychological study and, in fact, gives shifting impressions even of Joan's sexual nature that tend away from realism. If she appears sometimes sexual, still Baudricourt is able to suspect, at the start of the play, that Bertrand de Poulengey has a sexual interest in her, and, though she is "no beauty," she is deliberately associated with Dunois, "the brave Dunois, the handsome Dunois, the wonderful invincible Dunois, the darling of all the ladies, the beautiful bastard," who is cut out to be the romantic lead and lends her something of his own more conventional charm. In his company she appears unmistakably the most feminine creature in the play's sexual spectrum, perhaps something of a daughter-figure; though even here Shaw manages a sleight-of-hand with the lyrical scene on the banks of the Loire: there is a slight but definite touch of the troubadour about Dunois, as the blue flash of the kingfisher conspires to suggest that the coming of Joan to him, despite the disguise of her armour and bobbed hair and country bourgeois manner, has some quality of a visitation by the Virgin to her knight. "Mary in the blue snood, kingfisher color" is very weak poetry, and the whole scene verges perilously on whimsy, so that only its brevity in the playing can save it; but the conception is evident, and the kingfisher as a traditional symbol of Christ (as it is used by G. M. Hopkins) becomes an attribute of the androgynous Shavian saint. "Throughout the ages," A. J. L. Busst has remarked, "the mystical tradition has considered Christ an androgyne, from gnosticism through Jacob Boehme to Mme Blavatsky." Auguste Comte recommended the worship of Joan of Arc as an exceptional woman "whom theologians have been afraid to recognize" for "It was feared not without reason, that to consider Joan of Arc as a Saint might have the effect of spreading false and dangerous ideas of feminine duty." He argued the superiority of rational positivism over traditional religion on this basis: "So far from her apotheosis having an injurious effect on female character, it will afford an opportunity of pointing out the anomalous nature of her career, and the rarity of the conditions which alone could justify it. It is a fresh proof of the advantages accruing to Morality from the relative character of Positivism, which enables it to appreciate exceptional cases without weakening the rules." More subtly and deeply troubling than either a simply male or female figure could be, the Shavian ideal of human nature, which breaks so shimmeringly from the possibly wrong-headed simpleton, embraces the range from Saviour to heretic. But Joan, unlike Candida, represents an intellectual or moral danger, not an emotional danger. (Youth and inexperience leave the attractiveness of a daughter-figure untouched with the sinister, threatening quality invested in the more powerful mother.) Perhaps the chief source of difference between this play and most of Shaw's is contingent on the fact that no ambivalence is built into the character of the heroine: for once, the centre of the play *is* romantic and generous in feeling, not incorporating fear and dislike in however disguised a form.

Certainly Joan is a figure of the exploring spirit, single and free, not nurse, protector, and conserver of life. Shaw associates her with the air ("head in the sky"), with flight ("Are you afraid I will fly away?"), with freedom on the hills, in the light and the wind. The similarity between Joan's impulse towards such freedom and Barbara Undershaft's cry for the wings of a dove is significant: both are ideal figures, as well as idealists who need to work in partnership with practical men and in conditions of practical necessity. Joan's final cry marks her as an impossibilist, a utopian: "O God that madest this beautiful earth, when will it be ready to receive Thy saints? How long, O Lord, how long?" It is a formal, rhetorical close, the last flourish of the work of art; but it also marks the dramatist's release from the strain of maintaining throughout the play a necessary intellectual poise, committed in no direction, not even to irony. His own utopian impulse, already indulged in *Back to Methuselah,* would find new expression in the prophetic fables, the hypotheses of future history, that so largely occupied his last play-writing years.

Saint Joan:
Spiritual Epic as Tragicomedy

Charles A. Berst

The unique power of *Saint Joan* arises from its stress on factors which would seem to conflict with the legend of a saint, yet which undergird the legend through giving it a fresh, contentious, and broad context. Shaw subjects mysticism to rationalism, heroism to skepticism, villainy to understanding, and sanctity to humor, piercing traditional stereotypes with an irreverent, unrelenting scrutiny. The myth, far from being destroyed, is tested, and as it ultimately triumphs it emerges with a new energy and strength, having been rendered both credible and poignant on grounds which appeal to the modern imagination. The tale of Joan is vividly presented, but more intriguing is Shaw's penetrating conceptualization of the intrinsic nature of Joan, of the complex society in which she lived, and of their nearly epic interrelationship. While qualifying the supernatural with the human, Shaw links the human to great abstractions. He thereby vitalizes both myth and history with a twofold thrust, rendering them movingly alive through convincing human denominators and memorably significant through timeless social and spiritual implications. His undertaking, combining the immediacy of drama with a sensitive view of myth and a broad philosophical perspective of history, is a heroic attempt at a heroic totality. It incorporates both tragedy and comedy, which ultimately fuse in terms of compassionate understanding. To isolate the tragedy, the comedy, the myth, or the history, as have so many critics, is to distort his total achievement by

From *Bernard Shaw and the Art of Drama*. © 1973 by the Board of Trustees of the University of Illinois. University of Illinois Press, 1973.

partitioning it or by overemphasizing one aspect of a subtle complex. Responding to this complex, Luigi Pirandello was most apt when he described *Saint Joan* as "a work of poetry from beginning to end." Indeed, in its language, scope, cohesion, and inner dynamics the play involves poetry of a very bold and impressive sort.

Shaw's preface to *Saint Joan,* while extensively ramified by the play, is well worth a brief examination since it helps clarify germinal elements of his approach. Most notably, Shaw discusses the uniqueness of Joan, his particular artistic-historical viewpoint, and the "medievalism" or sense of allegory which distinguishes his dramatic method. His distinction of Joan as both genius and saint objectifies her nature on multiple levels. Joan as a personal figure takes on life as a "hardy managing type . . . a born boss . . . [a] combination of inept youth and academic ignorance with great natural capacity, push, courage, devotion, originality and oddity." When these qualities are combined, Joan's genius also becomes credible, with its "different set of ethical valuations" from the norm, valuations which contribute to her spectacular destiny. But most significant, and most haunting, is a sense that rationalists "will never catch Joan's likeness" because in her coalescence of drive, insight, personality, circumstance, and power there was "something more mystic," which Shaw describes as "forces at work which use individuals" for transcendent purposes—an "appetite for evolution, and therefore a superpersonal need."

We may not grant Shaw his specific terms, but as Joan emerges through his play we are likely to grant her an extra power which qualifies rational explanations with at least a covert sense of the supernatural. Thus he may call Joan's visions and voices illusory and describe her as a Galtonic visualizer, with "nothing peculiar about her except the vigor and scope of her mind and character, and the intensity of her vital energy," but in the accretion of her manifest capacities lies a hint of something transcendent which gives her a quality beyond genius. Shaw's ambivalence regarding this quality is suggested in the preface and grows in the play. Ironically, he creates a sense of Joan's mystical nature through his rational examination of the multiplicity of her genius. Her visions and voices may be only the result of a hyperactive imagination, but the inspiration she derives from them and her stunning achievements suggest forces at work which far transcend mundane humanity.

According to any conventional view of history, Shaw is certainly being blatantly anachronistic when in both the preface and the play he points up Protestantism, nationalism, and Napoleonic realism in Joan. These elements were obviously not articulated in any such manner in the early fifteenth century. However, as they symbolize elements in Joan's spirit and help objectify her actual influence on her environment, they serve as touchstones of understanding, touchstones which render Joan's medieval world more real by making it accessible and relevant to the modern mind. Critics who have objected to Shaw's lack of historicity have misappraised his method and missed the point of his drama. Shaw is striving for poetic truth rather than specific accuracy of fact—for a balanced, philosophical (and inevitably somewhat Shavian) comprehension of the times rather than for detailed verisimilitude. He acknowledges that Joan was a pious Catholic, but with the instinct of an artist he points up those unique elements in her which had implications far beyond the Catholic mold.

On his most vulnerable historical point—his assertion of Cauchon's fairness—Shaw remarks in his preface that "the writer of *high tragedy and comedy,* aiming at *the innermost attainable truth,* must needs *flatter* Cauchon nearly as much as the melodramatist vilifies him" (my italics). The purist may object, with good cause, that this is not truth, but the purist may be missing greater truths, since involvement in detail can so frequently obscure underlying principles. While Cauchon may have indeed played the role of a villain, such a category distorts him because it is no doubt at odds with his estimate of himself and because it stereotypes him in a pattern which emotionally obscures his historical position as a defender of the Church. For balance, both the personal and religious realities must be clearly presented and not melodramatized. Congruent to this vein, Shaw continues: "But it is *the business of the stage* to make its figures *more intelligible to themselves* than they would be in real life; for *by no other means can they be made intelligible to the audience. . . .* The play would be unintelligible if I had not endowed them with enough of this consciousness to enable them *to explain their attitude to the twentieth century* [with an] *inevitable sacrifice of verisimilitude*" (my italics). History is thus given meaning through art. In heightened self-awareness both individual characters and great abstract movements take on memorability through a poetic discipline involving concentration, selection, and dramatic patterning. Joan is subject to rationalism and her age is subjected to anachronistic terms, with both

Joan and her age becoming all the clearer as they transcend rationalism and anachronism on grounds which appeal to enduring levels of
spiritual and temporal understanding.

Shaw's medievalism, a quality which influences the philosophy
and structure of many of his dramas, is a central element in *Saint
Joan.* In comparing his play with those of Shakespeare, Shaw comments, "There is not a breath of medieval atmosphere in Shakespear's
histories," whereas "I have taken care to let the medieval atmosphere
blow through my play freely." Though he is indulging in overstate-
ment, his distinction between Shakespeare's Renaissance spirit and
his own is a key one. In *Richard II* Shakespeare typically explores the
depths of humanity in a king, while in *Saint Joan,* Joan's efforts are
to make a king out of a flawed human being. While Shakespeare
stresses the reality of the individual, Shaw stresses the reality of
abstractions, commenting that "a novice can read [Shakespeare's]
plays from one end to the other without learning that the world is
finally governed by forces expressing themselves in religions and
laws which make epochs rather than by vulgarly ambitious individuals who make rows." The case is surely not this simple, since the
problems of power are very much a concern of Shakespeare, just as
the problems of the vital individual are a concern of Shaw. But there
can be no doubt that the social-religious-political context prevails in
Shaw while the psychological context prevails in Shakespeare. As
Shaw perceptively delineates those great abstractions which impinge
upon the individual, his focus is less on a string of specialized human
encounters than on the great forces and patterns which bring about
life's recurrent tragedies and comedies. Insofar as the germ of man's
moral disease lies not just in the heart of the individual but in the
individual as influenced, mutated, or corrupted by the complexities
of his society, Shaw's emphasis is in this aspect more ambitious and
far-reaching. Ultimately he is both old fashioned and modern, caught
in the abstractions of the Middle Ages and the abstractions of the
twentieth century, imaginatively relating one to the other in hopes of
illuminating both.

Shaw's most Shakespearean character is Joan herself, who from
the very first distinctively thinks of people as individuals, an outlook
evidenced in her calling most men by their first names. One of
Shaw's alterations of history is to have Joan refer to the Dauphin as
"Charlie," whereas in fact she generally referred to him as "gentil

Dauphin." The dramatic objective is clear: to use given names is to equalize, to place all on a common human footing. The effect is to elevate Joan and to project her spiritual egalitarianism on the play, since as humans we are all children of God. Such an attitude in part accounts for Joan's direct power, but it is her fatal weakness as well, since she falters through failing to appreciate the grim reality of the abstractions behind individuals. The aesthetics of the play are in large part involved with the strength of her simplicity moving in counterpoint and contest with the stifling complexity of her society. As she ignores the latter, she rises meteorically, but as she does not understand it, it at last crushes her. In terms of spirit she is the stronger, but in terms of mankind which exists in spite of spirit, the social, religious, and political realities which surround her impose their mundane will. Joan, with her individualistic viewpoint, dramatically reveals both the power and the limitations of that viewpoint.

Joan's nature and status may be clarified by comparing her to Shaw's Caesar. Each represents a highly evolved manifestation of the Life Force, and the two have kinship as impressive historical phenomena whose genius serves as a context against which their respective worlds may be defined. Both are superhuman in a Nietzschean sense, since they create their own ethics, but while Joan is instinctive, unself-conscious, naïve, and spiritual, Caesar is rational, introspective, sophisticated, and transcendently moral. Their roles are similar in their great spiritual superiority, in their sense of spiritual isolation, and in their attempt to educate royalty to its responsibility. Caesar's power is both temporal and inspirational, but Joan's is mainly inspirational, and her tragedy has a different aspect from his. Caesar thoroughly understands his world, and his problem involves being caught in its schemes of sociopolitical vengeance despite his better instincts. Joan, on the other hand, is largely ignorant of the corrupt society which opposes her and is beaten by her ignorance as well as by her spirituality. Her tragedy is less internal than Caesar's, since she has not compromised herself in the world's terms. Hence the center of tragedy lies less in her personally than in the world which martyrs her. Powerful social, political, and religious abstractions bear the burden of guilt in proportion to the innocence of their victim, and in affairs of spirit the guilty are the most deeply tragic.

Shaw's method of dealing with these abstractions is as medieval as his subject matter—he fully exploits the potential shorthand, dramatic force, moral concern, and timeless emphasis of allegory. The aesthetic result is that his method fuses with his matter, augmenting the play's medieval atmosphere while providing it with a symbolic view of Joan, her world, and the ramifications of their interrelationship. Through this medium Shaw discerns basic, commonly neglected patterns in fragmentary historical events, patterns which reorient simplistic preconceptions regarding the Joan legend. The allegory ultimately gives a medieval mood to the play and a wide view of the age, besides giving an epic dimension to the characters, a poetic frame to the action, a point of reference clarifying historic and poetic ambiguities, and a context transcending time. On the other hand, the dramatic action vitalizes the allegory, making it memorable, especially through characters whose personalities are sharply individualized. Thus Joan has vibrant reality in a double sense: first, the romantic young victim of legend is personalized with a focus on her weakness as well as on her strengths; second, she is portrayed as a very real power in a historical situation which has symbolic permanence. Similarly, all of the characters have dramatic immediacy as contentious individuals with a mixture of personal virtues and vices, a mixture which upsets conventional stereotypes of them, while in a symbolic sense they represent great abstractions in an almost one-to-one relationship. In accordance with the issues of his allegory Shaw seeks to play up the spiritual drama while playing down the spectacle. In contrast to his directions regarding elaborate sets for *Caesar and Cleopatra,* he urged that the settings for the original production of *Saint Joan* be austerely simple. Against a neutral background the universal and timeless implications of Joan are allowed a simpler, purer expression.

The double vision which Shaw propounds in his preface, a vision sensitively perceiving both historical and allegorical reality, is carefully developed in terms of the insights and perspectives of the play. Through this vision Shaw evokes ambivalent sensibilities, qualifying material usually considered almost exclusively tragic. The conventional melodrama regarding Joan's fate is bypassed according to a deeper understanding which reorients fundamental assumptions regarding the mundane and the spiritual, the tragic and the comic. In this light Shaw's vision compounds itself, finally, into a six-fold view—historical, allegorical, mundane, spiritual, tragic, and comic.

All interlock in many illuminating and ironic relationships, but most notably the historical perspective is subject to allegory, the mundane perspective is primarily tragic, and the spiritual perspective is primarily comic. The play is structured to bring out the full implications of each of these elements, as they tend to develop in parallel, mutually relevant patterns. To trace the allegorical, tragic, and comic patterns and to be aware of their coalescence is to arrive at the heart of the play. As each pattern evolves through the nature of Joan, the nature of her opponents, the conflict between Joan and her opponents, and the outcome, the end result is a clear, compassionate comprehension of the Joan myth, a comprehension which is distinctive in combining a rational balance and dramatic power. Fictional renditions of Joan have traditionally suppressed the rational in pursuit of the dramatic, and, in the process, have achieved neither so successfully as has Shaw.

Allegorically and historically, the sainthood of Joan is tied to her genius, with the credibility of her mystical role linked to the precocity and power of her natural talents. Joan's genius has two main aspects: first is her undoubted ability, but equally important is her absolute commitment, integrity, and self-confidence regarding her cause, a cause she therefore asserts irrepressibly, despite awesome social obstacles. Her relentlessly directed singleness of purpose attracts a mystique of simplicity and moral strength which artfully complements the depth of her natural talents. Possessing this combination, her genius is kinetic and accumulates power as it meets resistance. In addition, Joan's genius involves what she believes she is, as well as what she represents. Appearing in the right place at the right time, her goals and her person do indeed promote and undergird a nationalistic spirit, as Cauchon observes in scene 4, just as her insistence on the divinity of her visions and on her personal right to determine their divinity forebodes Protestantism, as Warwick observes. Thus genius, moving through an indomitable will and a deceptive simplicity, forces its own terms on the world and accrues symbolic meaning and influence beyond its intention.

The issue of Joan's sainthood is developed through an impressive dramatic ambivalence in which skepticism complements conviction. Shaw builds the aesthetics of Joan's mystery by a subtle use of counterstatement. In scene 1 he has Joan herself interpret her voices as coming from her imagination, and in every successive scene he qualifies mysticism by offering a commonsense explanation through one character or another. Rationalism beats in constant counterpoint to mysticism. Ironically, the real mystery, through ultimately triumphing over rationalism, is thereby given a firmer, more convincing foundation. Despite the rational refrain, Joan's miracles accumulate throughout the play, numerically shattering coincidence and qualitatively confounding detraction. Frequently they are magical and fly in the face of their detractors, but the most significant miracles are usually those of Joan's supernal character as it triumphs repeatedly and most improbably against immense odds. When she wins over not only Poulengey and de Baudricourt, but also the rough Captain La Hire, the subtle Archbishop, the snivelling Dauphin, and the tough-minded Dunois, her other miracles seem almost inconsequential—but they are all definitely, hauntingly there, and the accretion overwhelms rationalism. The aesthetic effect of the rationalism is that of an argument which strengthens the case it opposes by being too insistently repeated in the face of impressive contrary evidence. Part of the grim humor of De Stogumber, Courcelles, and D'Estivet in the trial scene is less that their attribution of petty magic to Joan seems so improbable than that it is so trivial and insignificant when compared to her real powers, which impress us emotionally, if not logically, as supernatural and transcendent. Joan's genius and sainthood tend to fuse, informed most dynamically by the power of faith—her own faith in her cause, and her countrymen's faith in her divine inspiration. The miracle of her popular image and the poetry of her conviction coalesce with the fact of her accomplishments, routing skepticism. The old spiritual myth regarding Joan gains new life.

Confronting the spiritual force of Joan is the social, political, and religious world surrounding her, which Shaw objectifies through allegory. Shaw's allegorical scheme of the institutions of medieval society is impressive in scope and equally striking in its artistic condensation of so much complex material. The idea of the monarchy, with its powers, privileges, and weaknesses, he represents in the Dauphin. The aristocracy, corrupt, shallow, dull, and pompous, he represents in La Trémouille, Bluebeard, and the court. The petty aristocracy is present in de Baudricourt and Poulengey. The military, in its best, most pragmatic sense, finds voice in Dunois, while the army as a whole, simple, direct, superstitious, rough-speaking, is personified in La Hire. Warwick represents the feudal system; De Stogumber represents British nationalism. The Archbishop of

Rheims is a political prelate, representing the Church's combination of spiritual and temporal power; Cauchon represents the Church Militant, confronted by threats to its prerogatives; Ladvenu is the quiet spirit of compassion and altruism in the Church. The Inquisitor is the Inquisition at its theoretical best, while Courcelles and D'Estivet are the Inquisition at its ignorant, barbaric worst. The common people, being without organized influence, are offstage. Shaw thus carefully and economically portrays a wide strata of powers in the medieval world and, by testing them against so unusual and dynamic a phenomenon as Joan, probes the substance as well as the surface of the entire society.

The remarkable history of Joan's conflict with most of these forces is nearly allegorical in itself, and Shaw's achievement involves a pointing up of universals within the conflict. While each character has vital dramatic force on a personal level, sustaining the surface vigor and credibility of the drama, each has also to a large degree sold his soul to an abstraction. The institutions have codified vital thoughts, social desires, and spiritual aspirations into laws, mores, class distinctions, and a religious hierarchy. Free will is encompassed by numerous tyrannies, monsters largely of its own making, to which habit or self-interest has effected a slavish obeisance. When Joan's genius and saintliness confront this morass—with the impact of an irresistible force meeting an immovable obstacle—the struggle, like so many in Shaw, is bound to be archetypal and epic. The conflict involves a myriad of fundamental antagonisms: the young and the old, the vital and the stagnant, the spiritual and the mundane, the individual will and the collective ethic, the upstart and the social elite, the new faith and the old Church. As the conflict exposes the ossification and corruption of the institutions, Joan is in a very significant spiritual sense the winner. But when her spiritual victory is linked to her personal destruction at their hands, the result is grimly ironic. How is one to assess the ultimate historical and spiritual significance of geniuses and saints when their power is more spiritual than temporal and they are cruelly martyred by a race which is persistently, institutionally, barbaric? The influence of such as Joan echoes more in the inner consciousness of a few who truly understand, and only faintly if at all in the collective consciousness of the multitude. Time and the limits of the imagination transmute the great spiritual examples of sainthood into puerile superstitions, fairy tales, or, even worse, into new institutions. Historically and allegorically man ignores the meaning of his saints.

The tragic and comic patterns which grow out of Shaw's allegorical-historical view reveal a tight linkage of genres wherein the tragedy of man's blindness and folly frequently becomes indistinguishable from the comedy of that same blindness and folly. As these patterns reflect upon the allegory, the result is a tragicomic perception which transcends alternate emotions. In his preface, Shaw hints at basic elements of his approach, and incidentally acknowledges the artistic gap between preface and play which has plagued so much Shaw criticism: "This, I think, is all that we can now pretend to say about the prose of Joan's career. The romance of her rise, the tragedy of her execution, and the comedy of the attempts of posterity to make amends for that execution, belong to my play and not to my preface." Thus, according to Shaw, the play involves a poetry which rises above prefacing, and romance, tragedy, and comedy are all a part of that poetry. Later Shaw focuses more specifically on the martyrdom: "The tragedy of such murders is that they are not committed by murderers. They are judicial murders, pious murders; and this contradiction at once brings an element of comedy into the tragedy: the angels may weep at the murder, but the gods laugh at the murderers." In both quotations Shaw emphasizes the tragedy of the martyrdom and the comedy of man's relationship to it. In so doing he is touching on ambiguities of the play which go even deeper than he indicates. Several times he includes comedy and tragedy in the same phrase, finally asserting his "classical manner" in both genres. While it seems hardly likely that he can in one play have both classical comedy and classical tragedy, he does most remarkably cross-fertilize laughter, irony, and high seriousness according to patterns which suggest classical antecedents.

Historically and classically it would appear that tragedy prevails. Particularly in her role as a genius Joan's case suggests the pattern of Aristotelian tragedy, her fall resulting in part from hubris, in part from inexorable fate. It certainly arouses pity and terror and is to a great extent cathartic of these elements. In scene 5 the Archbishop specifically cites her hubris with reference to Greek tragedy; while his comment may result from personal animus, Shaw substantiates it throughout the play with a strong subtheme regarding Joan's pride. From scene 1 onward, Joan's scarcely modest identification with the will of God gives her both boldness and influence. When at the end of scene 2 she asks, "Who is for God and his Maid?" the question rings rhetorically, for who is against God? Such language is the property not only of saints, but also of bigots, fanatics, U.S. presidents, and tyrants. In the name of God and in a spirit which seems inextricably bound to an element of ego, Joan ascends in power. Shaw illustrates her growing hubris by opposing her awestruck humility before the Archbishop in scene 2—"[*She falls on both knees before him, with bowed head, not daring to look up*]"—to her insolent bluntness toward him in scene 5: "Then speak, you; and tell him that it is not God's will." As Joan's pride in wearing a gold surcoat brings about her capture, so her pride in defying the court hastens her martyrdom. Aristotelian tragedy moves like a ghost behind the action.

While a pattern of Aristotelian tragedy grows out of Joan's genius, a Promethean tragedy grows out of her saintliness. In asserting direct communion with divine forces, Joan threatens man's institutional gods by stealing their spiritual fire, fronting their self-assumed sanctity, and offering the dangerous ember of independent spiritual inspiration to all mankind. Her spark of divinity forebodes a blaze of insurgency, and forces of tradition and the status quo naturally feel it imperative both for their image and for their self-preservation that Joan's threat to them be adjudged heresy. The heretic is especially dangerous, since so much spiritual justice (and perhaps even God) is on her side. In the very strength of her virtue Joan is a challenge to society's estimate of itself, an estimate all the more tenacious and pompous because it is fundamentally petty. So, appropriate to Promethean legend, the vultures attack the saint, but the vital organ (in this case, Joan's heart) cannot be destroyed. Joan's foes, as fundamentally pagan as the avenging Zeus and his myopic vultures, cannot see that in destroying Joan physically they are immortalizing her spiritually. The unburnable heart is a phoenix symbol portending the renewal of Joan's spirit, purged and pure, from the ashes of her body.

The Promethean tragedy and the Aristotelian tragedy develop as diverse implications of a common set of facts, most simply being two ways of looking at the same event, but most profoundly representing two philosophical views—the optimistic, aspirational, and spiritual as opposed to the pessimistic, static, and mundane. The fact that the Promethean tragedy prevails, especially in light of the epilogue, means not that the Aristotelian tragedy is erased, but that it comprises a minor theme or counterpoint which renders Shaw's total statement more richly comprehensive. We have a sounder vision if we can acknowledge Joan's flaws while recognizing her inspiring spiritual example to her society. But as the conflict is Promethean, the focus of tragedy shifts away from Joan's person onto all mankind, past and present, represented by her self-centered, pragmatic, schismatic, doctrinal foes. Society, in judiciously murdering her, and in its conviction of the prudence and propriety of the murder, reveals its true decadence. And as the modern "monkey gland" mind finds itself superior to such inspiration as that provided by Joan, modern man partakes of the guilt of the murder. In Shaw's words, "For us to set up our condition as a standard of sanity, and declare Joan mad because she never condescended to it, is to prove that we are not only lost but irredeemable." Shaw indicates that a central problem of Joan's society and of our own is persistent mundanity, in which "rationalism" is an excuse for base vision and social conformity a haven from personal morality.

The conflict of repressive conventionalism and exuberant individualism is replete with tragic ironies. From a Christian as well as an Aristotelian point of view, the would-be saint's hubris and potential for tyranny have disturbing implications. How is one to be sufficiently selfless in the service of God so that he is sure his incentive is altruistic and divine, rather than egocentric and expressive of covert personal drives and ambitions? This is the dilemma which confronts Thomas Becket in T. S. Eliot's *Murder in the Cathedral* and which Eliot finally glosses over, answering symbolically in a manner which imposes only on the most gullible and blindly faithful. Symbolically, Becket surrenders his personal will to the greater will of God, but dramatically and dialectically he seems to be merely rationalizing a grotesque death wish, and the play's resolution, a supposed affirmation of faith, falls into rhetorical and poetic camouflage, concealing a spiritual evasion. Shaw's answer is more direct and satisfactory: the saint does not forgo personal will, but expresses God through it—as Joan's will is refined and noble, it is a natural outpouring of the divinity which informs all life. Hence there is little conflict, since hubris in the saint is at most a venial flaw, a by-product of ego, a secondary aspect of genius. Indeed, if hubris helps the saint's cause, it may well be a virtue. The problem of potential tyranny is far more serious, but is only hinted at in the play. As Joan gains great power through her identification with God, she is implicitly subject to the corruption that feeds on power. The cruelest of leaders have claimed divine sanction, and the most incredible barbarities, such as those of the Crusades and the Inquisition, have justified themselves in the name of God. By assuming too much, Joan is vulnerable. Hence Dunois's speech in scene 5, that "God is no man's daily drudge, and no maid's either." Joan's tragedy, which is closely tied to her virtue, lies partly in her inability to understand Dunois. In her accumulation of worldly power she is subject to the vanities and hazards of power politics, while in her naïveté she cannot deal with them effectively.

Even more strikingly, the conflict reveals manifold tragic ironies among those surrounding Joan. As her vigorous, assertive, independent presence places stress on timeworn institutions, the fallibilities of such institutions become starkly apparent. Were they unchallenged, the Church, the Inquisition, the feudal system, the court, and the king would each complacently presume to have its secure niche as a part of God's plan, its predestined link in His Great Chain of Being. Joan threatens these presumptions, transcending them according to her own system of values, and as these institutions are so profoundly affected by her in the temporal realm, they must account for her in the spiritual realm as well. The spiritual issue at stake is their own implicit or explicit claim to divine sanction, and the temporal issue involves their relative worldly influence. The fact that they are all rendered terribly uncomfortable by her, as she tends to level all men and to disorient tradition, reveals their intrinsic, very human weakness. Their repute is clearly less divine than man-made, and it rests upon a god made in man's image, congenial to man's systems, and generally more corrupt according to the degree of veneration he exacts. This god or, in his fragmented form, these gods are a central element in man's tragedy as they deflect man from a true spiritual awareness. Institutions have become a substitute for the spirit they claim to represent, and man, for the most part unconsciously, is damned by the baseness of his self-created false idols. As he serves them he becomes a wretched automaton, having surrendered his soul to a worldly power. Quite naturally, when a true saint comes along, the institutional man cannot recognize her, since his most fervent convictions are committed to what are in fact diabolical interests. Most simply we see this in De Stogumber, who has apotheosized nationalism and whose sense of spirit is caught in narrow chauvinism and petty superstition. Most complexly it is manifest in the subtle Inquisitor, whose uttermost charity is cruelty and whose doctrinal wisdom leads him to condemn as a heretic a young woman whom his church will later glorify as a saint. Institutional tragedy is thus fragmented into millions of little personal tragedies, all manifesting man's great hunger for respectability, a hunger which gnaws at his already finite spiritual sensibilities.

The power and scope of the tragedy, thus interpreted from historical record, is impressive. But the tragedy is primarily social, with a focus on the mundane, and there is a deeply founded comic refrain in the play which offsets its dark tones. Joan's Promethean nature tends to defy pessimism and to overwhelm the tragic pattern with a counterassertion rising forcefully from individual will and divine inspiration. Spiritually, there is a strong comic rhythm which both counterpoints and frequently coexists with the worldly tragedy, not entirely overwhelming it but profoundly transmuting its nature. Thus the genius of Joan, which develops on one level as hubris, leading her to her doom, develops on another level as spirited comedy, the humor of the nonconformist, filled with *élan vital,* opposed to convention, surprising, dismaying, and even at times overwhelming staid institutions and ossified modes of thought. Joan's spontaneity and pertness are irrepressible, prevailing from scene 1 through the horrors of the trial scene and bursting forth in the epilogue. They may be partly born of naïveté, but they are also born of a vital, optimistic principle underlying her nature; as she combines them with decisive action, they emerge as an aspect of her genius. With hubris evolving as pertness, the whole notion of Joan's Greek tragedy is qualified most quixotically by keen delight.

Concerning Joan's saintliness, the range of humor is even broader. In the first three scenes not even her miracles are allowed an exalted aura. From hens that will not lay and cows that hold back milk, to the drowning of Foul Mouthed Frank, to the obedient pennon, God seems to be guiding his saint with an earthy laughter. This strain is taken up once again as a leitmotiv in the dark moments of scene 6 with the piddling questions about magic spells, her voices' native tongue, and the Archangel Michael's attire—or lack of it. But more subliminal and basic is the intrinsic Christian consolation of spiritual rebirth, echoing the Resurrection, which transmutes Joan's Promethean tragedy into a Christian triumph. A spirit of transcendent comedy develops in a triple sense. First, as a Christian context accompanies the tragic pattern, the play's Greek pessimism cannot seem truly central, and its Promethean defiance takes on spiritual power. Second, Joan fulfills the classically comic role of youth confronting age, with youth ultimately prevailing. Third, in a strictly temporal sense, Joan's cause is won, as the English are driven out of France in the aftermath of her inspiration, and as her image in the popular memory obliterates her foes and immortalizes her as the true victor, an enduring ideal. Joan's final transcendence is a fundamental joke on her contemporaries and on all such deluded men, as it moves ironically in a timeless pattern, mocking conformity and institutionalism.

While the institutionalized men who desert or convict Joan are in their blindness and guilt actually more tragic than she, Shaw takes care to mitigate even their tragedy. The characters, being both distinctively allegorical and convincingly human, dramatically humanize the allegory. Thus Shaw has at the same time the significance and epic quality of the abstractions and the idiosyncrasy and triviality of their human representatives, with the space between the allegorical and personal providing special insights regarding both, setting a dramatic tone which incorporates the ponderous implications of the one and the vital dynamics of the other. The dichotomy destroys shallow notions of villainy by discriminating between abstractions that people follow, which may in effect be villainous, and the people themselves, who, like most human beings, feel honorable, kindly, and fundamentally well-intentioned. Shaw aptly remarks in his preface that a villain is a *diabolus ex machina,* two-dimensional, unreal—he is usually a confusion of a man with the role he plays. By discriminating between the man and the role while emphasizing the fact of both, Shaw's art combines a level of realistic drama with the consciousness of a morality. Thus some of his characters in the abstract may be villainous, menacing, and tragic, while concurrently as persons they are heroic, kindly, or even comic.

This double aspect is especially notable in De Stogumber, Warwick, Cauchon, and the Inquisitor. Politically, De Stogumber is a fervent nationalist, nearly as mad a bull as Sir John Talbot, a relentless, petty, cruel advocate of Joan's immolation; personally, he is a short-sighted, simple, rather comic man who would not harm a fly. Politically, Warwick is a ruthless and capable defender of the feudal system; personally, he is a cultured, sensitive gentleman with a suave, wry sense of humor. In an exceptional reversal of the pattern, Cauchon seems less admirable personally than officially. Ecclesiastically, he is a staunch, hard-line, but fair defender of the faith;

personally, his cleverness is offset by a hint of pomposity, and his sincerity is qualified by a tone of vengeful animus, possibly the result of his having been removed from his diocese by Joan's faction. More typically, the Inquisitor is a subtle, exacting, well-meaning but ironically cruel persecutor of saintly simpletons, while personally he is a type of kindly old uncle. Similar disparities between official capacity and personal nature exist in most of the other characters, being strikingly comic in de Baudricourt and the Dauphin. When the characters are not outrightly comic, the disparity in each of them renders them subtly so on a level of deeply ingrained incongruity. The disparity suggests that each has compromised his personal instincts in terms of an abstract standard; while this involves a tragic loss of soul, it concurrently suggests the implicit comic element of automatism, the humor of man as machine. In this latter sense the institutions themselves provoke a grim humor, being caught in rules, patterns, and laws which inaccurately apply to life, which time has rendered irrelevant, or which have virtue only in a mad inner consistency.

The very structure of *Saint Joan* serves as a vehicle for Shaw's tragicomic vision, graphically setting forth the archetypal, classically comic conflict between youth and age. In scenes 1 through 3 the spirit of youth, with its optimism, iconoclasm, innocence, and determination, is in the ascendency. The vital characters are all young— Joan is seventeen, the Dauphin and Dunois are both twenty-six. In these three scenes Joan rises through tests of increasing toughness. Each scene develops with society's skepticism, rational and cynical, being confronted and dazzled by Joan's assertiveness, and each scene ends with the skeptics at last won over to Joan's cause, enthusiastically concurring in the divinity of her mission. Through skepticism thus being dramatically overcome, Joan's miraculous nature is rendered all the more convincing and her cause all the more triumphant. Scene 3, undergirded by parallel elements in scenes 1 and 2, ends as a minor climax, the peak of the dramatic romance of Joan's ascendency. Following this the tone shifts drastically, suddenly moving away from spiritual exuberance and comedy toward mundane prudence and tragedy. Aesthetically the movement is from lightness to darkness, from youth to age. Warwick, Cauchon, and De Stogumber are all middle-aged, and it is their institutionalized world which takes over in scene 4, impressing its will upon Joan for the remainder of the play. The conflict evolves tragically toward the martyrdom of youth at the end of scene 6. But the epilogue at last shifts the entire tone as it brings together the vital spirituality of scenes 1 through 3 and the repressive mundanity of scenes 4 through 6. It is comic in the transcendence of Joan and in her reconciliation with society, since man retrospectively admires saints. But the reconciliation is ambiguous—negatively so, as society shies away from the idea of Joan's possible rebirth; positively so, in the very fact that saints will continue to appear in the world despite all odds against them.

While the structural pattern thus complements the allegorical, comic, and tragic patterns of the play, the individual scenes offer a constant accretion of details which energize the pattern with varying levels of consciousness. As these levels coexist and interact, they produce richly ambivalent drama. Most striking about the play's opening is that this rendition of a tale so frequently romanticized and sentimentalized begins on a tone of farce, the key joke of which is a miracle—hens which will not lay. The effect is cunning, first as the romantic tradition of the legend is at the outset countered by an irreverent tone, and, further, as one laughs at the inexplicable while one's laughter in no way removes an awareness that the event *is* inexplicable. A minor miracle is presented as fact, but the fact is conveyed in a mood of complete unpretentiousness. The simplicity of Shaw's description of Joan is in keeping with this double awareness, for through her seeming simplicity and naïveté arises a sense of profound strength. Joan's directness and audacity, flowing from a combination of absolute conviction and steadfastness, and covertly suggesting a suprarational ability, keep de Baudricourt off balance. He tries to categorize her—as a camp follower, as mad, as a victim of Poulengey's immoral intentions—but since she does not fit his categories, she easily disorients him, deflating his defenses and rendering him putty, especially with her incredible ambition to raise the siege at Orleans and to crown the Dauphin. The real miracle of the scene is that Joan wins her way, but even this is carefully prepared for by the portrayal of de Baudricourt as having *"no will of his own,"* and Poulengey as *"dreamily absent-minded"*—they are easy prey. Epitomizing the scene's double vision, Joan (quite unhistorically) admits that her voices come from her imagination, but nonetheless represent God's intention. Doubt plays in counterpoint with wonder most convincingly as Poulengey points up the miraculous essence of Joan: "I think the girl herself is a bit of a miracle. . . . We want a few mad people now. See where the same ones have landed us!" The halo which Joan sees around the head of de Baudricourt, causing him to look up apprehensively, catches the tension between humor and the miraculous which lends weight to his final exclamation: "She did come from God."

Joan's power, having moved the weak-willed and dreamy men of scene 1, faces a test far more severe in the Dauphin's court, which, though it is ripe for her in its irresolution and contentiousness, offers a much greater obstacle in the person of the clever, worldly Archbishop of Rheims. The likes of La Hire, a direct and earthy captain, and of the Dauphin, who delights in her as a new toy, may be easily impressed, but the Archbishop establishes a counterrefrain by rationally undercutting Joan's famous discovery of the Dauphin. His description of a miracle as "an event which creates faith," a nourishing of faith by poetry, subtly defines the tension between fact and imagination, rationalism and religion, which comprises an aspect of Joan's mystery. On a pragmatic level he senses her usefulness. His admiration of Pythagoras, who believed in a round earth revolving around the sun, indicates his sensitivity to very natural realities which seem incredible to less imaginative men. La Trémouille's response—"What an utter fool! Couldnt he use his eyes?"—typifies the rationalism of lesser men, a rationalism confined by the finite limits of their imagination. La Trémouille is the type to whom science is superstition and superstition is science. As such he is a precursor of modern man, inclined either to debunk Joan's voices as entirely impossible or to apotheosize them as strictly divine, unaware that there is a middle ground more impressive than either alternative. For once again Joan's ostensible miracles are overshadowed by her character, so direct, pure, and dedicated as to make the sophisticated Archbishop blush, and so stirring as to cause the ineffectual Dauphin to assert himself. With instinctive sharpness Joan realizes that the miracle of making the Dauphin into a king will be less one of crowning him than of changing his personality. As in *Caesar and Cleopatra* the prospect of such mundane sorcery borders on the supernatural, and, like Cleopatra, Charles's character changes less than his position. In a cutting observation of human nature Shaw later notes that Charles's true self-realization ultimately derives more from inspiration of the flesh than from inspiration of the spirit—Agnes Sorel, not Joan, makes him Charles the Victorious, much as Antony, not Caesar, brings forth Cleopatra the Queen.

Scene 3 is the climax of the spiritual-comic half of the play. Early themes culminate here, and rationalism is at this point shaken with a dramatic turn toward the miraculous. Dunois is more spontaneous and sensitive than the leaders Joan has previously encountered. He is a combination of pragmatist, poet, and believer, a man with *"no foolish illusions,"* but one who can appreciate the poetry of a kingfisher and the mystery of a saint. Like the Archbishop, his poetry complements his pragmatism, and, similar to Poulengey and La Hire before him, he recognizes Joan's inspirational importance, whether her voices be divine or not. He comments that Joan is in love with war, as the Archbishop had observed that she is in love with religion: Joan's dual loves render her a sort of latter-day Crusader, but Dunois wants a saint, not a daredevil. The fact that he has in Joan precisely what he is looking for is objectified by a poignant theatrical effect—that of the windswept pennon. Achieving in three dimensions the combination of simplicity and power which renders Joan's character so remarkable, the pennon is a device both dramaturgically audacious and psychologically forceful, serving to alter the entire supernatural emphasis of the play. Mounted on Dunois's lance, it stands out starkly on top of the single vertical prop on a horizontal landscape. The simplicity of the setting, a necessary aspect of so short a scene, and Dunois's vehement curse at the wind, which he emphasizes by shaking his fist at the pennon, doubly enforce the pennon's dramatic importance. It flutters in an east wind, almost possessing a personality, mute but assertive. After Dunois's opening speech the characters forget about it, but the audience obviously cannot, and when it droops suddenly at Joan's blazing entry it provides a stark, ironic comment on the ensuing dialogue. Once again a miraculous effect combines humor with wonder, but this time it is reinforced by being impressively visual, and by providing the audience with the dramatic and psychological relish of secret knowledge. As Joan and Dunois speak rationally about the logistics of warfare, they echo the chorus of rationalism which has the offset the miraculous up to this point—and all the while the pennon flutters in defiance of reason, in affirmation of faith, turning at last with a west wind. Dramatically and emotionally, if not logically, rationalism is at this point severely compromised, and when Dunois crosses himself, saying, "God has spoken," he echoes far more dynamically the conversion of de Baudricourt and the Archbishop in scenes 1 and 2. The issue has come to a tripartite conclusion, and, most movingly, the whole weight of this climax shifts conviction toward the supernatural.

While the characters of scene 3 are a boy, a seventeen-year-old, and a twenty-six-year-old, the characters of scene 4 are forty-six, fifty, and sixty. The reaction of age is juxtaposed to the action of youth; prudence and policy set themselves against optimism and exuberance. The scene's distinction lies in the fine economy, beauty, and forcefulness with which it conveys a great amount of complex material. Once again, reminiscent of the hell scene of *Man and Superman,* Shaw transmutes talk and a flux of ideas into highly energized, almost musical theater. He does this by scoring both the allegorical and personal levels according to emotional, rhetorical, and symbolic values which are nearly tonal. Thus Warwick, being suave, sophisticated, and imperturbable, with a voice which bridges the contentiousness of the other two men, suggests the quality of a lyric tenor, promoting feudalism with the social grace and subtlety of a consummate gentleman. Cauchon, by contrast, is pompous, dogmatic, and bombastic, with a voice ponderous and staid, suggesting the quality of a basso, defending the Church in a tone appropriate to its dignity, tradition, and divine pretensions. De Stogumber, finally, is excitable, bouncy, and impulsive with an intrusive and vehement voice, suggesting the quality of a comic baritone, asserting the cause of English nationalism in a manner exuding the fervor, narrowness, and self-righteousness of chauvinism. As these personalities, emotions, voices, ideas, and allegorical forces develop in counterpoint, the aesthetics of drama, music, and philosophy are brought into a stirring interrelationship. Neither Warwick nor Cauchon can brook Joan because she bypasses both feudal system and Church in terms of king and God, and her instinctive nationalism advances an institution which could severely diminish the power of peer and priest. As a royalist, Protestant, and nationalist, she is a harbinger of the end of their systems. So while they are by nature rivals, they join forces in a resolve to remove the threat. Their contrapuntal interaction throughout the scene, personally and allegorically contentious yet aimed at a common goal, develops with the immediate dramatic life of their characters, the tonal values of their interaction, and the epic overtones of the great abstractions which they so fervently represent. Thus the dialectic takes on the effectiveness of refined and powerful poetry.

The tragic pattern continues to unfold in scene 5, with a classical sense of fate inexorably closing in upon Joan. As scene 4 represented Joan's foes uniting in opposition to her, this scene reveals her "friends" deserting her. Ironically, the tragic situation has been largely of her own making and is inextricably bound to her success. Dunois touches upon a key cause in his question, "Do you expect stupid people to love you for shewing them up?" He attributes the court's hatred of Joan to jealousy, but even deeper than jealousy, no doubt, is the Establishment's humiliation at owing so much to a person so lowly. Sincere gratitude is hard on pride and is not the commonest of human emotions; human nature instinctively seeks to cancel it out, either by reciprocity or by finding fault in the benefactor. Being both small in charity and so very deeply in debt to Joan, her contemporaries naturally choose the latter course. Joan's essential spiritual nature has not greatly changed, but through her efforts the society around her has been materially rejuvenated. Hence that society denies her gratitude by condemning in victory those same qualities in her which it had found admirable during darker days—her voices, her love of war, her hubris. Joan's virtues are critically examined, and her divine inspiration is subjected to increasing rational doubts. Now that the miracle has been accomplished— the Dauphin crowned and the French reestablished—the saint who did it is an embarrassment and a nuisance. Almost inevitably, at the moment of her greatest triumph, Joan is symbolically deserted by King, Church, and Army. The effect is purgatorial, awakening Joan at last to an awareness of her true spiritual isolation, but as this isolation identifies her with Christ, she is all the more pure and transcendent. The ironies are multifold: Joan's temporal success brings temporal isolation, which in turn objectifies her spiritual triumph, though it portends her physical destruction. The tragedy of the world is implicit in the ignoble role it plays in making such ironies possible.

Scene 6 owes much of its effectiveness to the intrinsic humanness of its horror. Man's greatest tragedy has already been depicted in scenes 4 and 5, when he isolates Joan, rejecting her spirit and her God in the name of all of his personal, traditional, self-glorifying little gods. Now, in playing out his convictions, in justifying himself through tediously prosecuting one who is spiritually superior, man reveals the pathetic comedy which lies at the heart of his tragedy. The scene is especially distinctive as it brings together and clarifies at length the tragicomic disparity between man's highest spiritual achievement—his Church—and Joan's well-tested convictions. A spectrum of medieval Catholicism is represented—its subtlety, dignity, litigiousness, narrowness, foolishness, and compassion are manifest respectively in the Inquisitor, Cauchon, D'Estivet, Courcelles, De Stogumber, and Ladvenu. The institution, divine as it may profess to be, is laid bare as primarily a composite of those who make up its ranks; though it may have great power as an abstraction, that power is inextricably bound to the strengths, weaknesses, wisdom, and ignorance of its adherents. Shaw points up the tragic absurdity of the court's pretense by observing the foibles of its priestly constituency. In such a light the trial may be comprehended in more realistic terms— terrible as a conglomerate but pathetic in piecemeal and tragicomic in toto. The timeworn melodramatic stereotype of Joan's persecutors is destroyed. Indeed, melodramatic stereotyping is revealed to be one of the primary flaws of the persecutors themselves, as they subject life to their version of religion, religion which is a spiritual melodrama.

Thus despite its inherent tragedy scene 6 ranges from farce to irony. The pertness of Warwick's page at the opening sets an irreverent tone as he calls Cauchon "Pious Peter." This boy, providing a minor resurgence of the voice of youth, reflects the page of scene 2, who thumps assertively on the floor to gain the attention of the court, and Dunois's lively young page in scene 3, who is so naturally informal with his master. Warwick's fatherly tolerance toward the boy is but one of many strokes by which Shaw briefly but sharply gives dimension to character, and as Warwick addresses Cauchon and the Inquisitor, the mood of his boy's mockery is subtilized and extended in the nobleman's droll, pragmatic irony. The context of Warwick, who is present at the opening and closing of the scene, indicates that the court may play its games, but that they are really only games, in which the religious body is serving the ends of secular interests. Thus contextually circumscribed, the court's presumption of self-importance and seriousness is given a touch of Lilliputian absurdity, a touch which it fully lives up to as it goes into session. While Cauchon seeks to maintain fairness and dignity, De Stogumber pops up and down in his fanaticism, Courcelles promotes his petty six-four-count indictment, and D'Estivet urges a litigious formality. The air is filled with the farce of English-speaking Latin saints, a bishop's stolen horse, fairy trees, haunted wells, a rhetorically growing tower, and a naked archangel. Even threats of torture and cries of treason fall into a foolish pattern, putting Cauchon beside himself in irritation as the court's solemnity collapses. Joan does not help the situation, since she refuses to be impressed by tradition-bound dignity and follows the dictates both of divine voices and personal reason in a spontaneous defiance of her persecutors' sanctity. To the extent that she shocks the court, as she does most deeply, it appears all the more ridiculous.

But the farce is leavened by tragic irony, since these ridiculous men have the power to send Joan to the stake. With his usual sensitivity to visual effect Shaw dramatizes this fact in the person of the Executioner, who enters with Joan and stands like a shadow of death throughout her trial. Ladvenu brings about her temporary recantation by pointing out his presence. It is only at this point that Joan may be said to "fall"—in despair, ironically the one sin which was in fact regarded by the Middle Ages as truly unforgivable. Most impressive is the sophisticated, mild, kindly, treacherously benevolent Inquisitor, who, understanding Joan both in her innocence and in the terrible threat of that innocence to the Church, gently but firmly deprecates the foolishness of the others. One charge—heresy—is enough to burn her; while pleading compassion, righteousness, and mercy in terms of a greater cause—the cause of the Church, which is to him the cause of God—this man urges the inexorable point of ecclesiastical law and doctrinal common sense.

As the Inquisitor has the clearest sense of the religious factors, and as he follows them with a pure will, his personal irony is finally the deepest. He is the ultimate statement of spiritual authoritarianism, as opposed to Joan, the spiritual individualist. When Joan contends that "God must be served first. . . . What other judgment can I judge by but my own?" his response is implicit: the Church was created by God as His vehicle on earth; as the Church's judgment is derived from Him, you must abide by it. Both views are actually based on personal judgment, for it is, finally, the individual who always makes the choice in such matters. In the face of such an impasse one can only reasonably question whether it is indeed compassionate, righteous, and merciful to burn *anyone* for your own fervently held convictions. The weakness of the Inquisitor's case is suggested at the end when he and Cauchon seek "perfect order" in Joan's conviction, and when he admits that she is an "innocent creature crushed between these mighty forces, The Church and the Law." He has attached his spirit to a system and is willing to impose that system on others to the point of their death, despite his awareness of their personal innocence. Compassion is perverted into its opposite, and God's supposed cause must cruelly compromise itself in its very fulfillment. The ultimate conviction is the ultimate absurdity.

While irony is subtle and implicit in the Inquisitor, it is starkly dramatic and explicit in De Stogumber. Throughout scenes 4 and 5 De Stogumber is chafing to burn Joan, to the point of impatiently calling his superiors traitors for their compunctions. It is he who at last cues the Executioner—"Light your fire, man"—and helps push Joan out, exclaiming, "Into the fire with the witch." Humor is thus at its grimmest when he stumbles back after the burning, throws himself with a symbolic appropriateness on the prisoner's stool, and declares his soul guilty and damned. The terrible sight, smell, and emotion of the martyrdom have at last brought the reality of his barbaric impulses home to him. With emotional simplicity, again clearly symbolic, and providing a hint of the cyclic nature of such events, he identifies Joan with Jesus and himself with Judas. In his simple way De Stogumber has been shocked into compassion and understanding. He has borne graphic witness and has experienced a spiritual purgation in Joan's fire, a purgation which the Inquisitor cannot feel, being numbed by habit, and which Warwick avoids by staying away from the burning. The fact that the latter have greater sensibilities which they thus suppress implies that their state of mind, as well as their guilt, is even more damnable than De Stogumber's. They have the capacity to *know* what they are doing, but they do it anyway and insulate themselves from the consequences. The dark comedy, so clearly linked to tragedy and the macabre, rises in poignant grotesqueness as De Stogumber, with a singular consistency of character, thanks God that the man who gave Joan a cross at the end was an Englishman, and as he is desperately convinced that those who laughed were French.

De Stogumber's hysteria serves as a choric despair, but for deep tragic resolution a subtler tone is called for. Shaw stabilizes the concluding moments with the reentry of Ladvenu, who provides a sane, composed aesthetic balance. Ladvenu does not contradict the hysteria; rather, he affirms its cause and carries its implications a step further: "This is not the end for her, but the beginning." Ladvenu hopes the laughter was English. Humor and optimism are thus further entwined with the moment of tragedy and despair, serving to reduce the melodrama, to increase the human reality, and to give a philosophical perspective. The heart that would not burn serves as a final symbol of Joan's spiritual transcendence, the most haunting of the unexplained miracles, and a grim joke on her persecutors, one which Warwick appreciates *"with a wry smile"* as he echoes Ladvenu's words: "The last of her? Hmm! I wonder!" With comedy and trag-

edy joined, with the question of the miracles left dramatically ambiguous, and with Joan paralleled to Christ, the ending evokes a
spiritual power and poetic ambivalence which reverberate beyond
the fallen curtain.

Were *Saint Joan* only a historical account, the play might well
end at this point. Shaw, however, claimed that the epilogue was
necessary to show that Joan's history did not end with her martyrdom, but truly began with it. While this sounds simplistic, its ramifications are not. Aesthetically, the epilogue is a pastiche, primarily
comic, serving to offset the grim clouds of the preceding scenes with
a more dispassionate perspective. Beneath its levity is a fulfillment of
a spiritual rhythm through a ghostly resurrection in which a divine
force reasserts itself on mankind, producing a timeless spiritual lesson. As the play's concern is primarily with the interrelationship of
the mundane and the spiritual, reflected in the tragicomic nature of
man and the supernal nature of Joan, Shaw develops an allegorical
pattern which calls for a broad symbolic resolution. The epilogue
effects this resolution, immortalizing the nature of Joan's relationship
to man, forcing out its inner meaning and thereby propelling the
modern audience into the center of the play's spiritual implications.

Most notably, the epilogue dramatically refutes any comfortable
notion that *now* man is spiritually more enlightened than were Joan's
contemporaries. Man by nature is wisest in hindsight, lording over
history in retrospect. The fact that now we make Joan a saint and put
statues of her in cathedrals and in our city streets seems to speak for
the superiority of our civilization. But the epilogue graphically points
up the persistence of mankind's mundanity. By canonizing and by
erecting statues man sterilizes and crystallizes his saints, compliment-
ing himself that in freezing them as symbols he is both paying proper
homage and revealing his own state of grace. To the contrary, he
thus by and large puts his saints out of the way through converting
them to his own terms. Joan was removed by her contemporaries
through being immolated at the stake; she and her type are commonly removed by successive generations through being abstracted
and revered, transformed into a spiritual concept and example, and
consequently set in ice. Modern man, like medieval man, glories in
his dead Joans who, were they living, might well upset his self-
esteem, contradict his values, and endanger the status quo. In this
light Shaw opens and closes the epilogue with the rhetorical proposition of Joan's actual resurrection, a proposition followed by man's

inevitable response. Charles comments: "If you could bring her back to life, they would burn her again within six months, for all their present adoration of her." This assertion states the central theme of the epilogue, a theme which lurks ironically behind the universal praise of Joan—when all of the characters in turn kneel to her—and which emerges with pointed dramatic power when, in response to the praise, Joan asks, "Shall I rise from the dead, and come back to you a living woman?" The notion is dramatically, psychologically, and spiritually overwhelming, and the answer, of course, is that man wants his Joans in *spirit,* where he can pay lip service to them as an ideal, where they will serve as a noble example both of and to humanity and as a hopeful indication of God, but where, thank God, man will not have to *live* with them. Thus the characters slink away muttering apologies, and Joan is left as isolated as she was at the end of scene 5—a symbol of the glory of God, tragically, sheepishly, repeatedly avoided by mundane man.

The distinction between theoretical and actual spirituality is drawn most poignantly in De Stogumber. As a simple, direct exemplum revealing man's state, his significance rises above his limited nationalistic role to that of an Everyman. In the epilogue he emerges as an aged, senile version of the broken man who provided the real climax of the play itself. Now a beloved rector who is able to do a little good, a kind man who would not harm a fly, De Stogumber is portrayed touchingly and memorably through his drastic change from his former self. Unlike most of the others, his spiritual rejuvenation seems complete—not through Christ, who remains an abstraction, but through Joan, whose martyrdom was so intensely real: "Well, you see, I did a very cruel thing once because I did not know what cruelty was like. I had not seen it, you know. That is the great thing: you must see it. And then you are redeemed and saved." Cauchon's response touches the key of man's perennial spiritual tragedy, as it is represented in De Stogumber: "Must then a Christ perish in torment in every age to save those that have no imagination?" The answer lies in the nature of man and in his potential to draw perceptively and creatively upon his own spiritual resources. In the interim, Joan's question, "How long, O Lord," is open-ended.

Were man to possess any great degree of imagination, Shaw's epilogue would be unnecessary. But if Shaw had excluded it, his point would probably have been missed, since the total pattern would have been less clear. Shaw's contemporaries, no less than Joan's, had amply revealed their appalling lack of imagination. Modern man, tenaciously dense and worldly, by nature equally slow to think and quick to enshrine thoughtlessness, posed much the same problem for Shaw that medieval man did for Joan. The artist-reformer felt a certain kinship to the mystic-crusader in seeking to stimulate man's embryonic imagination to a deeper, braver, more spiritual under-standing. The major difficulty was age-old: how to vitalize abstract spirit, how to render it meaningful so that it might provide both a new conscience for man and a new base for decisive action. The answer in both cases was similar: to objectify by symbols, to wed artistry to theory, concretion to abstraction, poetry to inspiration, since to truly understand is to truly see, and ideas take on most poignant reality as they are tested, strained, and mutated by life. Not unlike a crusading saint, the great dramatic artist seeks to move men by being spiritually memorable, and to be spiritually memorable is to be both transcendent in insight and accessible in parable: "That is the great thing: you must see it. And then you are redeemed and saved."

The Saint and the Skeptic: Joan of Arc and George Bernard Shaw

William Searle

SHAW AND VITALISM

> *The moral government of God over the world is exercized through us, who*
> *are his ministers and persons, and a government of this description is the only*
> *one which can be observed as practically influencing men's conduct. God*
> *helps those who help themselves because in helping themselves they are*
> *helping him.*
>
> SAMUEL BUTLER, "God the Known and God the Unknown"
>
> *There are many scapegoats for our sins but the most popular is Prov.*
>
> MARK TWAIN, *Notebook 32*

Although Shaw's *Saint Joan* was not written until 1923, his interest in
religious heroism actually dates from a much earlier period. Twenty
years before, in complaining of the irreligiousness of Shakespeare
and Dickens, he remarked in the preface to *Man and Superman* that
"they are anarchical, and cannot balance their exposures of Angelo
and Dogberry, Sir Leicester Dedlock and Mr. Tite Barnacle, with
any portrait of a prophet or a worthy leader." He argued that, unlike
John Bunyan, who had "achieved virtue and courage by identifying
himself with the purpose of the world as he understood it,"
Shakespeare in particular was too much of a skeptic to succeed in

---

From *The Saint and the Skeptics: Joan of Arc in the Work of Mark Twain, Anatole France
and Bernard Shaw*. © 1976 by Wayne State University Press.

endowing his characters with that capacity for devotion to a transcendent objective which true heroism implies.

Shaw apparently developed this view of the dependence of heroic commitment upon religious conviction in reaction against the biological determinism of the followers of Darwin. The most objectionable feature of Darwinism, he believed, was precisely that it was anti-teleological: by representing evolution as the product of essentially blind and impersonal natural forces it had, in Samuel Butler's phrase, "banished mind from the universe." And in the process it had deprived men of that sense of metaphysical purpose which alone can nerve them to heroic undertakings. "Most of the natural selection men of the nineteenth century," Shaw declared in 1911, "were very brilliant, but they were cowards. We want to get back to men with some belief in the purpose of the universe, with determination to identify themselves with it and with the courage that comes from that."

Darwinism was not only irreligious, as Shaw perceived it, it was also fundamentally immoral, because its identification of competition as the sole source of evolutionary development tended to encourage the competitive spirit of capitalism at the expense of ethical idealism. "The theory of the survival of the fittest," he complained in 1912, "made the competitive system positively scientific." Nine years later, after the moral bankruptcy of that system had been glaringly exposed by the eruption of the most terrible war in history, he declared of Darwin's doctrine in the preface to *Back to Methuselah*, "If it be no blasphemy, but a truth of science, then the stars of heaven, the showers and dew, the winter and summer, the fire and heat, the mountains and hills, may no longer be called to exalt the Lord with us by praise: their work is to modify all things by blindly starving and murdering everything that is not lucky enough to survive in the universal struggle for hogwash."

Fortunately, Shaw argued, there are a number of excellent reasons for believing that Darwin's theory is not "a truth of science." And of these one of the best is the plain fact that many otherwise promising members of our species are subject to an "appetite for evolution" that is so far from being consistent with their will to survive that it often brings them to an early and violent end. The very existence of such an appetite, Shaw reasoned, is inexplicable in Darwinist terms—indeed, in any terms whatever that are not frankly metaphysical. Being neither material nor personal, it testifies to the pressure upon the psyche of forces that are both immaterial and superpersonal. It is apparently just this conviction that accounts for Shaw's interest in St. Joan; the reason for regarding her as a saint, he believed, is precisely that she herself was an embodiment of those immaterial forces.

Consequently, his characterization of her is imbued throughout by a conception of the essentially irrational, and therefore miraculous, character of heroic commitment. In the first scene, when Baudricourt asks whether he really believes that she can perform miracles, Poulengy responds, "I think the girl herself is a bit of a miracle." And he apparently reveals what he means by this remark when, shortly thereafter, he declares that "her words and her ardent faith in God have put fire into me." For the most impressive feature of Joan's character here lies in the obvious sincerity of her conviction that she is the agent of a divine purpose—a conviction which accounts not only for the "positiveness" with which she intimidates Baudricourt's steward, and the persuasiveness with which she wins over Baudricourt, but also, and most importantly, for the courage with which she faces the prospect of battle with the formidable goddams.

But however much of a "miracle" Shaw's Joan may be, she never succeeds in performing one, a fact which points up a fundamental difference between her conception of the God she is serving and that of her creator. God, as Shaw conceived him, is not a transcendent Being, capable of interfering in the orderly processes of nature. "What you have got to understand," he told a Christian audience in 1907, "is that somehow or other there is at the back of the universe a will, a life-force. You cannot think of him as a person, you have to think of him as a great purpose, a great will, and, furthermore, you have to think of him as engaged in a continual struggle to produce something higher and higher, to create organs to carry out his purpose; as wanting hands, and saying, 'I must create something with hands'; arriving at that very slowly, after innumerable experiments and innumerable mistakes, because this power must be proceeding as we proceed, because if there were any other way it would put us in that way."

Thus Shaw's "God," so far from being capable of interfering with nature on behalf of his creatures, is completely dependent on them. "It is not an omnipotent power that can do things without us," Shaw remarked of the life force in 1912; "it has created us in order that we might do its work. In fact, that is the way it does its work—through us." Accordingly, he completely rejected the Christian conception of the miraculous, arguing that irregularities in the orderly operation of natural law can only tend to the defeat of all natural foresight. He believed devoutly that nothing was impossible for the life force (hence his fondness for the expression "where there's a will there's a way"), but he held just as devoutly that events which are neither vitalist in origin nor rationally explicable must end by undermining our confidence in the sovereignty of the will over nature, and thus by subverting all meaningful religious faith.

In short, Shaw objected to Christian supernaturalism, not because it is credulous but because it is irreligious. "I think a man who is not Christian enough," he wrote in 1908, "to feel that conjuror's miracles are, on the part of a god, just what cheating at cards is on the part of a man . . . is not Christian at all." This idea clearly influenced his attitude toward the Maid. In the cathedral scene he allows Dunois to reproach her for relying too much upon such divine "cheating." "If you are worthy of it," he declares, "he will sometimes snatch you out of the jaws of death and set you on your feet again; but that is all: once on your feet you must fight with all your strength and all your craft. For he has to be fair to your enemy too; don't forget that." Shortly thereafter he adds, "I tell you that your little hour of miracles is over, and that from this time on he who plays the war game best will win—if the luck is on his side."

Moreover, Shaw had a more serious objection to Christian supernaturalism than that it tends to inspire such presumption. He also reasoned that it must have the effect of encouraging spiritual irresponsibility since as long as men are given to understand that they must depend for the welfare of their souls upon forces external to, and incalculable by, themselves, they cannot justifiably be held accountable for their own salvation. From this position he argued that the only sort of god whose nature is consistent with the fullest responsibility on the part of its worshipers is one who, like the life force, "possesses no executive powers of its own." Thus, in "The Religion of the British Empire," after asserting that he believed God, "in the popular acceptance of the word, to be completely powerless," he went on to repudiate the whole Christian ideal of resignation:

> If you don't do his work it won't be done: if you turn away
> from it, if you sit down and say, "Thy will be done," you

might as well be the most irreligious person on the face of the earth. But if you will stand by your God, if you will say, "My business is to do your will, my hands are your hands, my tongue is your tongue, my brain is your brain, I am here to do thy work, and I will do it," you will get rid of otherworldliness, you will get rid of all that religion which is made an excuse and a cloak for doing nothing.

Hence Shaw, in his play, rejected the Catholic view that Joan was endowed with supernatural powers, representing it in one of the work's most famous lines as the product of a medieval will to believe. In spite of the sympathy which he professes for the idea of miracles, he ended by explaining many of the miracles which have been attributed to his heroine as the results of an entirely natural exercise of her private judgment. After all, he seems to have reasoned, when every concession has been made to the truth that Man, far from being a mere machine, is "the Temple of the Holy Ghost," the fact remains that "it is only through his own brain and hand that this Holy Ghost . . . can help him in any way."

JOAN AS GALTONIC VISUALIZER

I have found again and again in my professional work that the images and ideas that dreams contain cannot possibly be explained solely in terms of memory. They have expressed new thoughts that have never yet reached the threshold of consciousness.

CARL JUNG, *Man and His Symbols*

Shaw is wrong when he claims in his preface that the nineteenth century concluded from Joan's voices that she was "mentally defective." On the contrary, the modern cult of the Maid coincides with the emergence of the romantic idea that the imagination is a principal source for our knowledge of reality. Yet Shaw, unlike such romantic admirers of Saints Catherine and Margaret as Michelet, rests his case for them largely on the unromantic claim that they gave Joan sound practical advice. Much of his discussion of the subject in his preface is devoted to an attempt to establish that claim on the basis of a scientific psychology.

In this attempt Shaw apparently relied heavily on the work of the English naturalist Sir Francis Galton. In his *Inquiries into Human Faculty and Its Development,* Galton asserts that there are a great many mentally healthy people whose visualizing faculty is so acute that it produces hallucinations, and that their failure to realize that they are hallucinating is not always evidence they are insane. He points out that highly imaginative children are often unable to distinguish between "the real and the visionary world"; whether they ever learn to do so often depends on the nature of their upbringing rather than on their mental and emotional stability. According to him, if such a child is raised among rationalists who regard his fancies as symptoms of mental disturbance, he will naturally take pains to identify and repress them; whereas, if he grows up in a climate of opinion which is favorable to supernaturalism, he will probably develop into a full-fledged seer. Under such conditions, Galton explains, "the faintly perceived fantasies of ordinary persons become invested by the authority of reverend men with a claim to serious regard, and they increase in definition by being habitually dwelt upon."

In this manner, then, the Maid's hallucinations may be accounted for merely by observing that she was born at a time when visionaries were encouraged, that her own visualizing faculty was very keen, and that her imagination had been deeply impressed by Christian iconography. "If Joan was mad," Shaw reasons in his preface, "all Christendom was mad too; for people who believe devoutly in the existence of celestial personages are every whit as mad in that sense as the people who think they see them."

How voices and visions may become vehicles of useful information, however, remains to be determined. Galton, among many case studies, cites none in which this was true, but he does suggest one means by which such a phenomenon may be explained. Distinguishing between hallucinations, which he calls "appearances wholly due to fancy," and illusions, which are "fanciful perceptions of objects actually seen," he remarks that "there is also a hybrid case which depends on fanciful visions fancifully perceived." He adds, "It is probable that much of what passes for hallucination proper belongs in reality to the hybrid case." Thus an "induced visual cloud or blur"—that is, one which has not been produced by an external impression—may be transformed by the imagination into what Galton calls a "fancy picture." When this phenomenon occurs in the case of an "illusion" such as that of a face seen in the fire, "this fancy picture is then dwelt upon; all that is incongruous with it becomes disregarded; while all deficiencies are supplied by the fantasy." From this it can easily be seen how the mind may come unconsciously to exercise control over the objects of the visualizing faculty:

> JOAN. . . . (*The cathedral clock chimes the quarter*) Hark! (*She becomes rapt*): Do you hear? "Dear-child-of-God": just what you said. At the half-hour they will say "Be-brave-go-on." At the three-quarters they will say "I-am-thy-Help." But it is at the hour, when the great bell goes after "God-will-save-France": it is then that St Margaret and St Catherine and sometimes even the blessed Michael will say things that I cannot tell before-hand. Then, oh then—
>
> DUNOIS (*interrupting her kindly but not sympathetically*): Then, Joan, we shall hear whatever we fancy in the booming of the bell.

Thus, according to Shaw, "Joan must be judged a sane woman in spite of her voices because they never gave her any advice that might not have come to her from her mother wit exactly as gravitation came to Newton."

Shaw seems, however, not to have been wholly satisfied with this prosaic explanation. After rejecting as "too vapidly commonplace" what he describes as the nineteenth-century account of Joan's voices, he asserts that the twentieth century "demands something more mystic," and adds, "I think the twentieth century is right, because an explanation which amounts to Joan being mentally defective instead of, as she obviously was, mentally excessive, will not wash." But in that case a major problem of the psychologist must be to determine how an illiterate country girl may come to be "mentally excessive" in the first place. It is easy to say that the "wisdom" of Joan's voices was "all Joan's own": the real problem, as Twain saw, lies in determining where she got that wisdom. Here Shaw could get no help from "modern investigators of human faculty." Galton does say that "the number of great men who have been once, twice, or more frequently subject to hallucinations is considerable." But he does not claim that their visions provided them with brilliant insights, much less explain the means by which such a phenomenon may occur. What was needed for that purpose, as Shaw perceived, was a theory of the creative process which would account for voices and visions as potential vehicles for inspiration. In providing such a theory he seems to have relied not on Galton's case studies but on his own researches into evolutionary biology.

The key to his rather complicated theory of vitalist inspiration is found in his account of the traditional conception of Satan. "It was a conception of enormous value," he told an audience of heretics in 1911, "for the devil was always represented as a person who could do nothing by himself, and that he had to tempt people to do wrong." He explained that in this respect Satan resembles the God of vitalism, who, being similarly powerless to compel his agents, had also hit upon the device of tempting them in order to get them to fulfill his purposes. "If we conceive of God as working in that way," he added, "and having a tremendous struggle with a great, whirling mass of matter, civilization means our molding this mass to our own purposes and will, and in doing that really molding it to the will of God."

What gives this conception its "enormous value," then, is that it provides an answer to the question how "a bodiless, impotent force, having no executive power of its own" can nevertheless get its work done in the world. "Temptation and inspiration mean the same thing," Shaw declared in this connection, "exactly as firmness and obstinacy mean the same thing, only people use the one word when they want to be complimentary and the other when they want to be abusive." The hallucinatory character of Satan was also of service here because it indicated a precise psychological means by which organisms may be tempted to strive for conditions which do not yet exist, and thus pointed to a solution to the very difficult problem of identifying the origin of variation in species.

How serious a problem this was in terms of the evolutionary theory of the day is revealed by an examination of the sources of Shavian vitalism. Samuel Butler, in *Evolution Old and New,* had urged as part of his attack on Darwin the objection that "natural selection cannot be considered a cause of variation . . . for the variations must make their appearance before they can be selected." "Suppose that it is an advantage to a horse," Butler explains, "to have an especially hard and broad hoof, then a horse born with such a hoof will indeed probably survive in the struggle for existence, but he was not born with the larger and harder hoof *because of his subsequently surviv-ing.* . . . The variation must arise first and be preserved afterwards." Yet as cogent as this objection must have seemed at the time, Butler was aware that in this matter he was no better off than Darwin. His theory of the hereditary transmission of "unconscious memory" will indeed account for the preservation of acquired faculties, but it will not explain how such faculties come to be acquired in the first place. "We can no more have an action than a creative effort of the imag-ination cut off from memory," he declares; but how in that case can an organism learn to do anything which was not already done by its ancestors? Shaw was later to present this conundrum in terms of the Eden myth: women know how to give birth because they are daugh-ters of Eve; but how did Eve herself know?

Moreover, Henri Bergson, whose influence on Shaw's vitalist ideas was second only to Butler's, was struck by the same difficulty. He urges it in support of his irrationalist attack upon the intellect:

> It is of the essence of reasoning to shut us up in the circle
> of the given. . . . If we had never seen a man swim, we
> might say that swimming is an impossible thing, inasmuch
> as, to learn to swim, we must begin by holding ourselves
> up in the water and, consequently, already know how to
> swim.

For Bergson it is "action" which enables us "to cut the knot which reasoning has tied" in this case. He explains, "But if, quite simply, I throw myself into the water without fear, I may keep myself up well enough at first by merely struggling, and gradually adapt myself to the new environment." But Shaw reasoned, in ef-fect, that there is more to such action than is implied by Bergson's description. Before one throws himself into the water, he must want to learn to swim. And as motivation is by definition a goal-directed function, he must begin by imagining something which does not yet exist, namely, himself as a swimmer. Hence Bergson's solution really begs the question; although we may have no difficulty imag-ining ourselves swimming if we have already seen someone doing it, this condition is obviously not met by the original swimmer. Is Butler wrong, then, when he claims that we cannot have "a creative effort of the imagination cut off from memory"?

Shaw apparently found the answer in his experience as a playwright. In a letter to the *New York Times,* June 2, 1912, he replied to a request to identify "the principles which govern the dramatist":

> I am not governed by principles; I am inspired, how or why I cannot explain, because I do not know; but inspiration it must be; for it comes to me without any reference to my own ends or interests.
>
> I find myself possessed of a theme in the following manner. I am pushed by a natural need to set to work to write down the conversations that come into my head unaccountably. At first I hardly know the speakers, and cannot find names for them. Then they become more and more familiar, and I learn their names. Finally I come to know them very well, and discover what it is they are driving at, and why they have said and done the things I have been moved to set down.
>
> This is not being "guided by principles": it is hallucination; and sane hallucination is what we call play or drama.

Long before writing *Saint Joan,* then, Shaw had a personal motive for wanting to learn how and why the imagination dramatizes its intuitions. A careful study of this passage reveals much about the extent to which his vitalist theory is indebted to his dramatic practice. It is clear, for instance, that an impulse which comes to an individual "without reference to his own ends or interests" cannot plausibly be attributed to Darwinian natural selection, and Shaw's use of the word *inspiration* in this context suggests that "a creative effort of the imagination" can in fact come to us from sources which lie outside the range of Butlerian racial memory. Moreover, although the nature of those sources is not explained in the passage itself, the "natural need" to which it refers is clearly biological, and the fact that it is a "superpersonal" rather than a private need suggests that it must be a need of evolution. Thus the life force, like the God of Christianity, is able to enlighten the understanding of its agents without the aid of their physical senses. "The garden is full of voices sometimes," Eve remarks in the first part of *Back to Methuselah.* "They put all sorts of thoughts into my head." By having Joan tell Baudricourt that it is through the imagination that the messages of God come to us, Shaw easily evaded the ontological confusions to which Joan's voices had condemned Twain.

Shaw's view that the voices were analogous to the creations of great imaginative writers is not especially original; it may be found, for example, in Michelet. But Shaw's vitalism allowed him to go much farther than Michelet in defining the analogy between hallucination and poetry, for it allowed him to derive, from the romantic doctrine of inspiration which they shared in common, an aesthetic which virtually identifies artistic creation with organic process.

The clearest exposition of Shaw's organic theory of art is Godfrey Kneller's verbal assault on Sir Isaac Newton in Shaw's drama *In Good King Charles's Golden Days* (written 1939). Kneller begins by denying that the normal path of a moving body is a straight line. After all, he reasons, although he is "the greatest draughtsman in Europe," even he cannot draw such a line without a ruler, and God does not own a ruler. Moreover, even if He did He would not use it; for, as the straight line is a "dead thing," a cosmos made of it would be a mere piece of mechanical gadgetry instead of the clearly inspired piece of craftsmanship which every good artist perceives it to be: "The line drawn by the artist's hand, the line that flows, that strikes, that speaks, that reveals! that is the line that shows the divine handiwork."

This suggests that among the characteristics which are shared in common by artistic and organic techniques of creation are freedom and spontaneity. In developing this idea Shaw appears to be relying on Bergson. Distinguishing between two kinds of order, Bergson at one point remarks, "The order of the second kind may be defined as geometry, which is its extreme limit; more generally, it is that kind of order that is concerned whenever a relation of necessary determination is found between causes and effects. It evokes ideas of inertia, of passivity, of automatism." But, he continues, the order of the first kind—that of vital phenomena—eschews both geometry and mechanism: "Of a free action or a work of art we may say that they show a perfect order, and yet they can only be expressed in terms of ideas approximately, and after the event. Life in its entirety, regarded as creative evolution, is something analogous."

Hence, Bergson concludes, scientific attempts to explain vital phenomena, to the extent that they rely upon mathematical abstraction, necessarily lead to distortion. To this position Shaw adds that the artist, because his methods are the same as nature's, may normally be expected to anticipate the findings of the scientist. "Your Majesty: the world must learn from its artists because God made the world as an artist," Kneller at one point declares. "Your philosophers steal all their boasted discoveries from the artists; and then pretend they have deduced them from figures which they call equations, invented for that dishonest purpose."

In short, Shaw held that inspiration is in general a more reliable source of new data than ratiocination, and that it normally precedes it. In answer to Dunois's remark that he would think that Joan were "a bit cracked" if she weren't able to give him sensible reasons for what she did, Joan replies, "Well, I have to find reasons for you, because you do not believe in my voices. But the voices come first; and I find the reasons after; whatever you may choose to believe." Yet, as Shaw recognized, the use of the method of inspiration is by no means a guarantee of success either in art or in science. Even if one accepts his view that "all truths, ancient or modern, are divinely inspired," one may still object, as he does, that "the instrument on which the inspiring force plays may be a very faulty one, and may even end, like Bunyan in The Holy War, by making the most ridiculous nonsense of his message." Similarly, Shaw's use of the phrase "sane hallucination" to characterize drama is open to serious objection, for, as he frequently insists, most drama, like most visualizing, is merely escapist. What was still needed then—and what Michelet in fact had failed to provide—was an objective criterion for distinguishing between hallucinations which are sane and those which are merely the result of mental infirmity.

In furnishing such a criterion, Shaw may well have been influenced by Schopenhauer. He argues in The World as Will and Representation that "Imagination has been rightly recognized as an essential element of genius" since it "extends the mental horizon of the genius beyond the objects that actually present themselves to his person." But it does not follow, he adds, that "strength of imagination" is "evidence of genius." For just as a real object can be considered in two ways—either idealistically as it is in itself, or practically as it relates to other objects and to the will of the individual thinker—so also, can an imaginary one:

> Considered in the first way, it is a means to knowledge of the Idea, the communication of which is the work of art. In the second case, the imaginary object is used to build castles in the air, congenial to selfishness and to one's own whim, which for the moment delude and delight. . . . The man who indulges in this game is a dreamer; he will easily

mingle with reality the pictures that delight his solitude, and will thus become unfit for real life.

Similarly, Shaw advances three criteria to identify a hallucination as "sane." First, it will enable the mind to transcend the limitations imposed upon it by its dependence on perception; second, it will come to one "without reference to his own ends of interests"; finally, being to that extent free from subjective distortion, it will not unfit one for constructive action in the real world. Thus, in 1914, in "Parents and Children," the preface to *Misalliance,* he distinguished two kinds of imagination: the "romantic," which he describes contemptuously as "the power to imagine things as they are not"; and the "realistic," which is "the power to imagine things as they are without actually sensing them." "The wise man," he explains, "knows that imagination is not only a means of pleasing himself and beguiling tedious hours with romances and fairy tales and fools' paradises . . . but also a means of foreseeing and being prepared for realities as yet unexperienced, and of testing the feasibility and desirability of serious Utopias."

Some years later Shaw presented the results of this inquiry into the imagination and its role in evolution in his "metabiological Pentateuch" *Back to Methuselah* (written 1918 to 1920). He suggests that since "there is no such thing as the future until it is the present," the "realistic imagination" necessarily plays a vital role in all acts of creativity and invention. The hero—or rather heroine—of the first part of the work is the serpent, whom Shaw characteristically identifies with inspiration. Being a mother herself she informs Eve of what one must do to give birth by asserting that "imagination is the beginning of creation." Before a thing can be created, she explains, it must first be desired; and since it does not yet exist, the imagination alone is capable of making it an object of desire. "You imagine what you desire: you will what you imagine; and at last you create what you will," she declares; and she points out in the same context that Eve originated in the mind of Lilith through "a marvelous story of something that never happened to a Lilith that never was."

The serpent then describes such stories as poems, implying that nature's methods of creation are the same as those of poets. Hence the soundest insights into natural process are to be derived not from scientific textbooks but from "inspired human language." In the second part of the "Pentateuch," the enlightened vitalist theologian

Franklyn Barnabas asserts, "The poem is our real clue to biological science." "The most scientific document we possess at present," he explains, "is . . . the story of the Garden of Eden." By using that story to indicate that natural birth was "invented" by the life force in order to prepare life for "the pursuit of omnipotence and omniscience," Barnabas provides another valuable hint concerning the nature of the harmony which subsists between literary creation and organic process. As the method of the life force is the method of inspiration, so the fruits of the womb and those of the muse are alike in being expressions of the aspiration of life toward the unlimited perfection of God.

This is the position Shaw had reached by 1920. Three years later he argued from it that "the figure Joan recognized as St Catherine was not really St Catherine, but the dramatization by Joan's imagination of that pressure upon her of the driving force that is behind evolution which I have just called the evolutionary appetite." His experience as a dramatist, reinforced by his vitalist convictions, had carried him far beyond Galton to a highly original mystique of the role of the imagination in history.

Shavian History

Nicholas Grene

There is a story (apocryphal no doubt) of a Cecil B. de Mille epic in which the troops were roused by the stirring line, "Men of the Middle Ages, let us now rise up and go out and fight the Hundred Years War." Anachronism is of the essence in any dramatisation of history. We can only see what we can from where we are. To us the Middle Ages are the Middle Ages, after the Dark Ages, before the Renaissance; however little aware the soldiers at Crécy or Poitiers were of the fact, we know that the war they were fighting was to last on and off for roughly a hundred years. To ask modern actors to play the parts of historical figures, to write for them lines which will be intelligible to contemporary audiences, to make of the complicated and half-known facts of the past an immediate and dramatic present is and must be anachronism enacted. Indeed, one of the commonest forms of inauthenticity in historical drama derives from a superficial concern with the accurate recreation of period. Scrupulously faithful costumes and décor, careful historical background research, can often do no more than make us aware that what we are watching is a shell of past action conspicuously empty of reality. If the history play or film is going to convince us, it must create its own reality which lives in our here and now.

But with the greatest history plays—and in English this means Shakespeare and nobody else—there is a profound sense of an encounter with the past. We all know the jokes about the conspirators in *Julius Caesar* with their very un-Roman hats plucked down over

From *Bernard Shaw: A Critical View*. © 1984 by Nicholas Grene. Macmillan, 1984.

their faces. Yet T. S. Eliot was surely right when he argued that "Shakespeare acquired more essential history from Plutarch than most men could from the whole British Museum." The Roman tragedies are very much plays of their own time, but they represent a vision of Roman history which is not merely a projection backwards of Renaissance England. There is in *Coriolanus* a vivid evocation of the atmosphere of the emergent republic, in *Julius Caesar* and *Antony and Cleopatra* a compelling view of the power politics through which the republic was turned into the empire. Whether or not they represent historical truth, the plays show us Shakespeare's imagination inhabiting a milieu which is indentifiably not his own, reaching out to a past which he authenticates by his capacity to imagine it.

Shaw in *Saint Joan* measured himself against Shakespeare, not obtrusively and aggressively as in *Caesar and Cleopatra,* but without diffidence either. In the preface he explained his procedure in conceiving the historical characters who surrounded Joan: "I really knew no more about these men and their circle than Shakespear knew about Falconbridge and the Duke of Austria, or about Macbeth and Macduff. In view of the things they did in history, and have to do again in the play, I can only invent appropriate characters for them in Shakespear's manner." But, he went on to claim, he was in a position to understand the medieval period as Shakespeare, living still too close to it in time, never could. That understanding, moreover, was an understanding of the significance of historical events which, he complained, Shakespeare never attempted: "a novice can read his plays from one end to the other without learning that the world is finally governed by forces expressing themselves in religions and laws which make epochs rather than by vulgarly ambitious individuals who make rows." His *Saint Joan* was to be more than a Shakespearean clash of characters, much more than a conventional costume drama:

> Those who see it performed will not mistake the startling result it records for a mere personal accident. They will have before them not only the visible and human puppets, but the Church, the Inquisition, the Feudal System, with divine inspiration always beating against their too inelastic limits: all more terrible in their dramatic force than any of

the little mortal figures clanking about in plate armor or moving silently in the frocks and hoods of the order of St Dominic.

Shaw's object was to write a play in which what he took to be the historical significance of the life of the fifteenth-century saint would be manifest to a twentieth-century audience. What sort of dramatic reality was the result?

One answer is supplied in the preface, where Shaw speaks of *Saint Joan* as showing "the romance of her rise, the tragedy of her execution, and the comedy of the attempts of posterity to make amends for that execution." The play is in turn romance, tragedy, and comedy, the three modes corresponding to its three movements: scenes 1–3 concerned with the rise of Joan up to the climax of the relief of the siege of Orléans; scenes 4–6 showing not only the trial and execution but the chain of circumstances which led up to it; and the epilogue which evokes the five-hundred-year-long rehabilitation which ended with Joan's canonisation in 1920. To try to define the quality of *Saint Joan,* we need to consider the nature of these three modes and movements and how far they blend together to give us something which is both genuinely Shaw and genuinely a play about Joan of Arc.

Again and again in the preface and elsewhere, Shaw stressed that in writing the play he had done no more than dramatise the transcript of her trial and the later fifteenth-century enquiry which reversed the trial's verdict: "I took the only documents that are of the smallest value—the report of the process and that of the rehabilitation. I simply arranged what I found there for the stage, relying on Joan to pull me through, which she did." This is, of course, Shavian over-statement, but Brian Tyson has made clear how very closely Shaw did stick to his main source, T. Douglas Murray's edited and trans-lated version of J. E. J. Quicherat's *Procès de Jeanne d'Arc.* In return-ing to the original documents, in rejecting the romantic legends which had grown up about Joan, Shaw felt that he could realise upon the stage the much more dramatic drama of the real-life events.

To a large extent, therefore, even the romance of Joan's rise to power which is represented in the first three scenes of the play is intended to be antiromantic romance. Joan, Shaw stresses, was not good-looking, not the beautiful Maid of perfervid imagination. Tak-ing as his model instead the head of St Maurice in Orléans, reputedly a portrait of Joan, he describes her as having "an uncommon face: eyes very wide apart and bulging as they often do in very imaginative people, a long well-shaped nose with wide nostrils, a short upper lip, resolute but full-lipped mouth, and handsome fighting chin." Jeanne, from Lorraine in the North of France, in Shaw becomes a rough-speaking country girl with a somewhat dubious north-country dialect. Most annoyingly, and most unconvincingly, Shaw gives to Joan the mannerism which he so frequently gives to his masterful young women, that of calling the other characters by nicknames. Just as Octavius Robinson and Roebuck Ramsden are Ann's Tavy and Granny, as Adolphus Cusins and Charles Lomax become Barbara's Salvation Army recruits Dolly and Cholly, so Joan makes a Jack of Sieur Jean de Metz, a Polly of Bertrand de Poulengy, and a Charlie of the Dauphin. The more resounding the name, the more Shaw delights in reducing it to a nursery-like familiarity which bespeaks the effortless and humiliating control exercised by his strong heroines.

Throughout Shaw is bent on demystifying the figure of Joan. She is to be seen as plain-speaking, buoyant, unabashed, unreverent. Shaw could never conceive "a great man as a grave man," and his Saint Joan, as much as his Caesar, was to have little time for conventional gravity. But Eric Bentley is exactly right when he claims that Shaw's intention was not only to "show Joan as a credible human being" but to "make her *greatness* credible." He was determined to remove the glamour of the legendary Joan because by making her apparently ordinary, he could all the more effectively highlight what was truly extraordinary in her character—the energy, the resolution, the unswerving will. Throughout the first three scenes of the play, the romance section, we see her steadily imposing her will on others. Robert de Baudricourt, her first and easiest victim, is characterised as "handsome and physically energetic, but with no will of his own" and when the play opens he "is disguising that defect in his usual fashion by storming terribly at his steward." The unfortunate steward, with his deficient hens, is there to represent the bottom of a heap which Joan will swiftly climb to the top. In the second scene her success is all the more remarkable because it is the Dauphin, with his tenacious instinct for survival by the line of least resistance, whom she must inspire with her fighting spirit. There is a significant replay in the interview between Joan and the Dauphin of the encounter between Caesar and Cleopatra. Just as Caesar taught

Cleopatra queenliness, Joan, by a similar mixture of harrying and coaxing, gives the Dauphin a crash course in kingliness. Both are lessons in the use of the will. But the reversal of roles, by which it is the adolescent girl who teaches the older man, makes Joan's achievement all the more striking and enforces Shaw's point that the vital genius, the figure of outstanding will, may appear in any human shape or form.

In the opening scenes of the play Shaw thus goes far towards establishing Joan as an antiromantic Shavian superwoman. Yet he does not altogether deny to the audience the Maid of romance with her voices and miracles. The voices were clearly a problem for Shaw, as he made clear in the preface:

> I cannot believe, nor, if I could, could I expect all my readers to believe, as Joan did, that three ocularly visible well dressed persons, named respectively Saint Catherine, Saint Margaret, and Saint Michael, came down from heaven and gave her certain instructions with which they were charged by God for her. Not that such a belief would be more improbable or fantastic than some modern beliefs which we all swallow; but there are fashions and family habits in belief, and it happens that, my fashion being Victorian and my family habit Protestant, I find myself unable to attach any such objective validity to the form of Joan's visions.

Shaw accordingly interpreted the voices as "the dramatisation by Joan's imagination of that pressure upon her of the driving force that is behind evolution." In the opening scene he shows Joan herself aware of this interpretation:

> JOAN: I hear voices telling me what to do. They come from God.
> ROBERT: They come from your imagination.
> JOAN: Of course. That is how the messages of God come to us.

And later she admits that they may be "only echoes of my own commonsense." But there can be little doubt that Jeanne d'Arc believed in her communication with the saints at a much more literal level than this. At her trial attempts were made to suggest that she suffered from hallucinations brought about by fasting, or even perhaps from erotic fantasies which might be the sign of demonic possession (as in the authentic question, which Shaw borrows, about whether St Michael appeared to her as a naked man), but Jeanne countered them all with solidly detailed testimony as to the nature of her supernatural visitations. There is an uneasy tension within *Saint Joan* between the representation of the historical Joan's real belief in her voices and Shaw's desire to credit her with something more like his own rationalistic attitude.

Shaw's treatment of Joan's miracles is even more ambiguous, and in some ways less defensible. The Archbishop of Rheims in the second scene gives a nonmiraculous account of miracles. He explains to La Trémouille in advance that Joan will be able to spot the substitution of Gilles de Rais for the Dauphin: "She will know what everybody in Chinon knows: that the Dauphin is the meanest-looking and worst-dressed figure in the Court, and that the man with the blue beard is Gilles de Rais." But this, he goes on to add, will not make it any less of a miracle.

> A miracle, my friend, is an event which creates faith. That is the purpose and nature of miracles. They may seem very wonderful to the people who witness them, and very simple to those who perform them. That does not matter: if they confirm or create faith they are true miracles.

This concept of the miracle as a faith-creating conjuring trick might seem to be Shaw's own. Several critics have assumed that we are not intended to accept Joan's miracles at their face value, but instead to witness their effect on those more credulous than ourselves. However, when we consider the dramatic use to which the miracles are put, it is hard to sustain this view.

The miracle of the eggs in the first scene was, as Shaw himself explained, an invention to take the place of the real event which convinced or converted Robert de Baudricourt:

> The apparent miracle which impressed him was the news of the Battle of Herrings. Joan learnt this from the mouth to mouth wireless of the peasantry. She was therefore able to tell him what had happened several days before the news reached him by the official routine of mounted messenger. This seemed to him miraculous. A much simpler

form of miracle has been substituted in the play to save tedious and unnecessary explanations.

In giving a sceptical explanation of the real-life "miracle" here, Shaw would seem to imply that the invented substitute is of a similar order. But this is hardly the effect of the strong ending of the first scene:

> *The steward runs in with a basket.*
> STEWARD: Sir, sir—
> ROBERT: What now?
> STEWARD: The hens are laying like mad, sir. Five dozen eggs!
> ROBERT (*stiffens convulsively; crosses himself; and forms with his pale lips the words*): Christ in heaven! (*Aloud but breathless*) She did come from God.

This is pure ham, but it is surely unironic ham, intended to send shivers of excitement up the spine in the theatre. Similarly with the changing of the wind before Orléans in scene 3.

> DUNOIS (*looking at the pennon*): The wind has changed. (*He crosses himself*) God has spoken. (*Kneeling and handing his baton to Joan*) You command the king's army. I am your soldier.

In performance it is impossible to respond at this moment with sceptical detachment, to smile at Dunois's naiveté (he is not naive) in seeing supernatural meaning in a natural event. To claim that Shaw, at moments like these, is "satirising popular religious psychology" is like the neoclassical critics who defended Homer's (otherwise improper) inclusion of the marvellous in *The Odyssey* by explaining that all those stories of the Cyclops and the Sirens were simply fantasies invented by Odysseus for the benefit of the gullible Phaeacians.

Each of the first three scenes of *Saint Joan* ends with a similar high-point, as the miracles of the Maid create faith in those around her. The audience is surely intended to share this excitement. And yet at some level we must be affected by Shaw's partial scepticism, his awareness that what he is writing is "romance." Sybil Thorndike recounts how when Shaw first read the play to her, after she had listened spell-bound to the opening three scenes, he remarked "That's all flapdoodle up to there—just 'theatre' to get you interested—now the play begins." One suspects that the comment may have been partly a matter of embarrassment at the romantic nature of these scenes, but there is nevertheless a damning ring of truth to it. The romance section of the play is skilfully crafted—Shaw had not worked in the theatre for thirty years for nothing—but, with its blend of farcical comedy and drama, its atmospheric kingfishers on the Loire, it seems often more a knowing exploitation of theatricality than an action of real dramatic integrity.

And Shaw's real business does begin in scene 4. The tent scene is a brilliant and wholly Shavian invention which is crucial to the play's structure. It gives Joan herself a much-needed break from the stage and in her absence makes possible a broad and generalising discussion of the meaning of her life (and in anticipation) of her death. Shaw chooses for his interlocutors the Earl of Warwick, who commanded the English forces at the time of Joan's capture and execution, and the Bishop of Beauvais, who presided over her trial. They represent in this scene the viewpoint of the feudal nobility and of the Church, as Shaw saw it, the two great forces to which Joan was opposed. They are characterised only to the limited extent that they need to be contrasted. It scarcely matters if we agree with Desmond MacCarthy that Warwick "is a purely eighteenth-century nobleman." There is no effort made to pretend that Cauchon and Warwick are "in period" in this scene; rather they self-consciously expound what they are about in a conversation which is necessarily out of normal historical time. The principle involved is the cardinal one for Shaw, advanced in the preface: "it is the business of the stage to make its figures more intelligible to themselves than they would be in real life; for by no other means can they be made intelligible to the audience." The third party to the conversation in the tent scene, the English chaplain De Stogumber, has been very commonly written off as one of Shaw's mistakes in the play. However irritating we may find Shaw's crude and silly caricature of the chauvinist Englishman, he does to some extent turn that irritation to account by making of De Stogumber the butt of Cauchon and Warwick as well as our butt, by using his clownish interruptions to vary and punctuate the main formal debate.

The purpose of the debate is to establish the essential principles of Protestantism and nationalism for which Shaw claimed Joan stood. In a cleverly choreographed dialogue, Warwick the feudalist and Cauchon the Catholic churchman diagnose the two ideas associated with Joan which they are resolved to combat. On the one hand, as

Warwick says, there is "the protest of the individual soul against the interference of priest or peer between the private man and his God. I should call it Protestantism if I had to find a name for it." On the other, as Cauchon puts it, for Joan "the French-speaking people are what the Holy Scriptures describe as a nation. Call this side of her heresy Nationalism if you will." There were, inevitably, protests against this interpretation of Shaw's as eccentric and wildy anachronistic, but he had more than a little support for it in his source. He might well have taken his cue for Joan's nationalism from a comment in T. Douglas Murray's introduction:

> Nations in the modern sense had not fully arisen. The State was everything. Whether a great Anglo-French monarchy sitting in Paris ruled over France, England, Ireland, and Wales, or a more domestic French line only ruled over France itself, was a question on which upright men might well take opposite sides. Jeanne's special merit was that she saw the possibility of a great French nation, self-centred, self-sufficient, and she so stamped this message on the French heart that its characters have never faded.

Her "Protestantism" is illustrated on page after page of the transcript of her trial, as she refused categorically to accept that the Church Militant was a higher authority than her own sense of her divine mission. When she was asked, "Will you submit your actions and words to the decision of the Church?" she replied, "My words and deeds are all in God's hands: in all I wait upon him"; or again:

> "Will you refer yourself to the decision of the Church?"
> "I refer myself to God Who sent me, to our Lady, and to all the Saints in Paradise. And in my opinion it is all one, God and the Church; and one should make no difficulty about it."

The rehabilitation enquiry was at pains to try to establish that Joan had been willing to submit her case to the Pope or to a General Council of the Church, refusing to accept the judgement only of the ecclesiastical court, which was packed with her political enemies. This was the view, also, of Shaw's friend the Irish priest, Father Leonard, who acted as his "technical adviser" while he was writing the play. But the occasional references in the trial itself to the possibility of an appeal to the Pope appear to be ambiguous at best, and there is much to support Shaw's reading of Joan as unable to accept any authority which would deny the truth of her personal inspiration by God.

Whether we accept Joan as protonationalist, proto-Protestant or not, there is a remarkable detachment in the presentation of the arguments in the tent scene. Shaw has perhaps relatively little real sympathy for Warwick's point of view, the feudal barons' fear of a centralised monarchy which would break their power deriving from Joan's idea of the king as God's deputy, but Warwick is allowed to present it articulately and with force. But to Cauchon the Catholic, Shaw gives real eloquence:

> What will the world be like when The Church's accumu-lated wisdom and knowledge and experience, its councils of learned, venerable pious men, are thrust into the kennel by every ignorant laborer or dairy-maid whom the devil can puff up with the monstrous self-conceit of being di-rectly inspired from heaven? It will be a world of blood, of fury, of devastation, of each man striving for his own hand: in the end a world wrecked back into barbarism.

With all the "holy wars" of the Reformation and Counter-Reformation to look back on, not to mention the nationalist conflicts which had culminated in Shaw's day in the First World War, the identification of Joan as Protestant and nationalist was no doubt intended to give us pause. Robert Whitman scarcely puts it too strongly when he says that Shaw's Joan appears as the "saint of emergent capitalism." And yet we are made to feel that the attitude of Cauchon and Warwick, however deeply understandable, is a re-actionary one, and that the spirit of Joan, however terrible its his-torical consequences, must be supported against them. Shaw was an internationalist politically, and the medieval idea of a supranational state and church should have had much to recommend it to him. Elsewhere in his work, most notably in *John Bull's Other Island,* he appeals to a concept of fully catholic Catholicism transcending na-tional barriers as an ultimate ideal. But he resisted the common nineteenth-century socialist tendency to sentimentalise medieval feu-dalism, and instead celebrated Joan as one of those exceptional his-torical figures whose mission is to move the world on, even it was to move it on to other terrible eras.

If scene 4 shows us the full force of Joan's enemies and what they stood for, scene 5 gives the equivalent picture of how little support she was to expect from her friends. Just as he left Joan immediately before the triumph of the relief of Orléans, it was a real dramatist's instinct which made Shaw return to her in Rheims cathedral immediately after the great climax of the crowning of the Dauphin. With Joan praying in the empty cathedral, we catch a glimpse of a private moment between two public shows, the coronation and the appearance to the people outside. In this behind the scenes atmosphere, Shaw builds up naturally and effectively the sense of her isolation. Once again the individual characters who warn Joan stand for more than themselves. If she is captured, she will not have the support of the monarchy—Charles will not ransom her; though the Archbishop of Rheims is on her side politically, he will not use the authority of the Church to help her against Cauchon and the Inquisition; Dunois, her closest friend and companion in arms, yet speaks firmly for the army that he will not risk the life of a single soldier to save her. With immense skill Shaw creates out of the individual voices a formal chorus of renunciation.

That chorus is designed to bring out the developing emotions of Joan. She begins in the affectionate intimacy of a conversation with Dunois who, for all his feeling for her, cannot really understand when she tries to tell him about her voices: "You make me uneasy when you talk about your voices: I should think you were a bit cracked if I hadnt noticed that you give me very sensible reasons for what you do, though I hear you telling others you are only obeying Madame Saint Catherine." To which Joan can only retort "crossly," "Well, I have to find reasons for you, because you do not believe in my voices. But the voices come first; and I find the reasons after: whatever you may choose to believe." It is almost as though in Dunois Shaw parodied his own inclination to rationalise Joan's voices—he too uses the mocking "Madame Saint Catherine" in the preface. The relationship between Joan and Dunois remains an affectionate one, but limited in understanding. When they are joined by the other main characters, Joan makes a rather half-hearted offer to the King to return to her village now her mission to crown him in Rheims has been accomplished, and is visibly hurt and taken aback by the alacrity with which the offer is accepted. She is stung to vociferous and belligerent opposition by talk of treaties and an unwillingness on the part of the French to press home the advantages she has won for them. She attacks the faint-hearts with rough arrogance: "I tell you, Bastard, your art of war is no use, because your knights are no good for real fighting." It is only by degrees that she registers the full force of the animus against her and her arguments, and in the rhetorical clash the other voices in the chorus come to dominate hers. She is horrified and bewildered by the threats that are made against her.

And yet out of that horror and bewilderment, out of the realisation that she is alone, she draws the strength which is expressed in one of the greatest speeches in Shaw. It must be quoted at length:

> Yes: I am alone on earth: I have always been alone. My father told my brothers to drown me if I would not stay to mind his sheep while France was bleeding to death: France might perish if only our lambs were safe. I thought France would have friends at the court of the king of France; and I find only wolves fighting for pieces of her poor torn body. I thought God would have friends everywhere, because He is the friend of everyone; and in my innocence I believed that you who now cast me out would be like strong towers to keep harm from me. But I am wiser now; and nobody is any the worse for being wiser. Do not think you can frighten me by telling me that I am alone. France is alone; and God is alone; and what is my loneliness before the loneliness of my country and my God? I see now that the loneliness of God is his strength: what would He be if He listened to your jealous little counsels? Well, my loneliness shall be my strength too; it is better to be alone with God: His friendship will not fail me, nor His counsel, nor His love. In His strength I will dare, and dare, and dare, until I die. I will not go out now to the common people, and let the love in their eyes comfort me for the hate in yours. You will all be glad to see me burnt; but if I go through the fire I shall go through it to their hearts for ever and ever. And so, God be with me!

The scriptural echoes of so much of this speech are made all the more effective for the development of the pastoral image from literal to metaphorical level. The two main rhetorical movements are separated by a nicely judged piece of commonsensical colloquialism: "But I am wiser now; and nobody is any the worse for being wiser." The

touch of childish petulance—"You will all be glad to see me burnt"—
is turned into a ringing affirmation of the meaning of martyrdom. It
is here that we truly see what Shaw meant by calling Joan a Protestant. As Brian Tyson has pointed out, the speech draws upon the
final lines of Stockmann in *An Enemy of the People,* "the strongest
man in the world is he who stands most alone." There is a strain of
absolute individualism in Ibsen, however hedged round with ironies
it may be in the figure of Stockmann, and it is this Protestant individualist stance which Shaw attributes to Joan: "it is better to be
alone with God."

In the trial scene Shaw did, very nearly, what he claimed he had
done, that is to dramatise and arrange the events, even the very
words, which he found in the original documents. Many of the
questions and many of Joan's replies are taken all but verbatim from
Murray and, though Joan's recantation and subsequent retraction of
the recantation happened over a period of days, what Shaw gives is
only a theatrically heightened image of what actually took place. The
main Shavian invention in the trial scene is the figure of the Inquisitor and the immensely long speech he is given in defence of his role.
Shaw's insistence, against all the traditional prejudices, that the judges
who tried Joan were fair-minded and reasonable men is, of course,
one of the key features of the play and provoked the most controversy (as no doubt it was intended to do). The Inquisitor's apologia
might seem to be the ultimate achievement in Shavian devil's advo-
cacy. Certainly T. Douglas Murray, his main source from whom he
derived so much, took the conventional view of the authorities who
tried Joan. "The worst of these servile churchmen was the wretched
Bishop of Beauvais, Pierre Cauchon. Many other prelates were
Caesar's friends, but he sits exalted in solitary infamy." Yet it was
not merely perversity which made Shaw try to reverse this verdict
on Joan's accusers. Reading through the account of the trial and the
rehabilitation enquiry, one can see why Shaw saw it as he did. There
can be little doubt that the Bishop of Beauvais, as supporter of the
English, under constant pressure to find Jeanne guilty, must have to
some extent been biased against her. Yet the trial lasted over three
months, Jeanne was very comprehensively examined and frequently
exhorted to repent, and though some anecdotal evidence suggests
that Cauchon was determined to find a means to convict her even
after the recantation, there is also a suggestion—on which Shaw
built—that he refused to act merely as an ecclesiastical stooge for the

English. It was not a kangaroo-court that tried Jeanne d'Arc; if it was, obviously, in some sense a political trial, the rehabilitation proceedings were every bit as political, perhaps more evidently bent on redeeming the reputation of Jeanne than the original judges were on convicting her.

Shaw acknowledged in the preface that he flattered the character of Cauchon, virtually invented the character of the Inquisitor, who is a very shadowy figure in the account of the trial. But he argues that such were the "inevitable flatteries of tragedy," that in order to make the trial of Joan fully significant, he had to make her judges the best possible representatives of the system that found her guilty:

> It is, I repeat, what normally innocent people do that concerns us; and if Joan had not been burnt by normally innocent people in the energy of their righteousness her death at their hands would have no more significance than the Tokyo earthquake, which burnt a great many maidens. The tragedy of such murders is that they are not committed by murderers. They are judicial murders, pious murders; and this contradiction at once brings an element of comedy into the tragedy.

This is a very significant passage. It is typical of Shaw in his refusal to be interested in evil, his belief that most of what is wrong in the world is caused by misguided people acting according to their lights. It explains why he lavishes on Cauchon and the Inquisitor such evident sincerity, such reasoning force and eloquence. They are serious men who fervently believe in their principles; they are only terribly, tragically mistaken. And yet, as Shaw admits, there is comedy in that tragic conviction and in the clarity with which it is seen. One of Shaw's greatest comic gifts was to show the inevitable clash of impenetrable argumentative attitudes. In the trial scene in *Saint Joan* he put that comic gift to the service of tragedy:

> CAUCHON: . . . Joan: I am going to put a most solemn question to you. Take care how you answer; for your life and salvation are at stake on it. Will you for all you have said and done, be it good or bad, accept the judgement of God's Church on earth? More especially as to the acts and words that are imputed to you in this

> trial by the Promoter here, will you submit your case
> to the inspired interpretation of the Church Militant?
> JOAN: I am a faithful child of the Church. I will obey the
> Church—
> CAUCHON (*hopefully leaning forward*): You will?
> JOAN: —provided it does not command anything impos-
> sible.
>
> *Cauchon sinks back in his chair with a heavy sigh. The
> Inquisitor purses his lips and frowns. Ladvenu shakes his
> head pitifully.*

Joan's reply here is taken more or less directly from the trial transcript—"On all that I am asked I will refer to the Church Militant,
provided they do not command anything impossible." But Shaw in
building up the solemnity of Cauchon's question, in breaking Joan's
reply, makes of this a moment of anticlimax which is basically a
comic technique. Joan cannot understand what seems so appallingly
heretical to the judges in what she has said; the judges cannot for a
moment enter into Joan's view of things. In another context we
might be able to laugh; here the gap in understanding is too wide, the
consequences too terrible, to make it a laughing matter.

Shaw talks of the tragedy of Joan's execution, coming after the
romance of her rise. Is it in fact tragedy as he represents it? It has been
a much argued question. The common view at the time of the play's
first production was that Shaw, for once, had written a true tragedy,
but had then ruined it by the addition of his comic excrescence of an
epilogue. Arland Ussher has argued just the opposite, that it is rather
the burning of Joan which is anomalous, out of key with the rest of
the play, and that the purpose of the epilogue is "in fact, to restore
the easy argumentative note which the intrusion of the brutal historical facts has a little disturbed." This is perhaps somewhat un-
fair—the clash of irreconcilable points of view in the trial is in some
sense experienced as a tragic clash—but it is true to the extent that
Shaw is unwilling to face the full horror of Joan's execution. He
could never bear really to imagine the idea of pain, and one of the
reasons that he opposed what he called "Crosstianity" so vigorously
was that he could not accept suffering as redemptive. It is not acci-
dental, therefore, that he chooses to register the effect of the burning
through the buffoon turned grotesque figure of De Stogumber. The
English Chaplain, the most vehement opponent of Joan, who earlier

declared his willingness to burn her with his own hands, is utterly horrified by the sight itself. His broken and hysterical words are intended to demonstrate the degree to which cruelty is merely lack of imagination. But this is hardly a full apprehension of the tragic nature of Joan's death, and Shaw keeps De Stogumber's comic chauvinism to the end: "Some of the people laughed at her. They would have laughed at Christ. They were French people, my lord: I know they were French." We pity De Stogumber, we are even moved by his conversion, but we are left with enough detachment to smile at his unconverted partisanship.

From the moment of Joan's exit at the end of the trial, we can see Shaw tuning the play back towards the serio-comic tone of the epilogue. Even the appearance of the Executioner involves a joke (lifted directly from Shakespeare's Abhorson in *Measure for Measure*):

> WARWICK: Well, fellow: who are you?
> THE EXECUTIONER (*with dignity*): I am not addressed as fellow, my lord. I am the Master Executioner of Rouen: it is a highly skilled mystery.

At certain moments Shaw is prepared to risk drastically lessening the impact of the trial we have witnessed in order to achieve this retuning of tone. As Cauchon is about to hurry out to stop the English dragging Joan straight to the stake without formal sentence by the secular authorities (as they in fact did), the Inquisitor holds him back: "We have proceeded in perfect order. If the English choose to put themselves in the wrong, it is not our business to put them in the right. A flaw in the procedure may be useful later on: one never knows." There is a similar effect with the last line of the scene; when the Executioner assures Warwick that he has "heard the last of her," he replies, "The last of her? Hm! I wonder!" Shaw here prepares us for the reappearance of Joan in the epilogue, prepares us for the continuation of her story into the "comedy of the attempts of posterity to make amends" to her. But the knowingness of these lines given to the Inquisitor and to Warwick seems a real indecorum in context. The whole force of the trial scene depends on the assumption that Joan's judges, and the Inquisitor especially, are men of complete probity. The suggestion that in fact the Inquisitor has one eye on the future when a technical loophole might be desirable, surely comes close to sabotaging altogether the integrity of the character. There is a theatrical slickness in Warwick's curtain line which again seems to betray the seriousness of what we have just seen. Shaw's irresistible urge to turn his characters into smart alecs rarely served him worse.

The epilogue was essential to the play from Shaw's point of view: "I could hardly be expected to stultify myself by implying that Joan's history in the world ended unhappily with her execution, instead of beginning there. It was necessary by hook or crook to shew the canonised Joan as well as the incinerated one." And hence we get a dream-sequence like that in *Man and Superman* with a similar comic eschatology: the Soldier describing the jolliness of Hell—"Like as if you were always drunk without the trouble and expense of drinking. Tip top company too: emperors and popes and kings and all sorts." This vein of schoolboy facetiousness, so irritating and yet in a way rather endearing, is very characteristic of Shaw. The English soldier, in fact, had figured in his first fantastic sketch of what he might do with a Joan play—"beginning with the sweeping up of the cinders and orange peel *after* her martyrdom, and going on with Joan's arrival in heaven." The epilogue is antitragic in that it allows us to escape the finality of death, so fundamental to the sense of tragedy, into a region of cosy immortality in which the characters can congregate amicably to discuss the action.

But the epilogue is not merely Shaw the joker taking over after the self-restraint of the tragic drama. There is more to it than the opportunity for Joan to exchange bantering repartee with all the other characters, to give her shrewd comments on all that happened after her death. It is a real attempt to show Joan's tragedy in the ultimate light of divine comedy. The epilogue is intended as a salute to the spirit of Joan and what it achieved both in the short term—the freeing of France and the firm establishment of Charles VI on the throne—and in the long term—the inspiration to later generations recognised finally in the canonisation in 1920. This is formally expressed in the litany of praise from her assembled friends and enemies who kneel to her, in thanks for showing them their limitations. But this is followed by a deliberate anticlimax:

JOAN: . . . And now tell me: shall I rise from the dead, and come back to you a living woman,
A sudden darkness blots out the walls of the room as they all spring to their feet in consternation.

One by one, in a pattern of denial to match the previous paean of praise, they refuse to accept the idea of her return. Shaw's design here is to repeat in little the basic structure of the play as a whole: the inspiring force of Joan which occupies the first half, met by the worldly sources which in the second half doom her to death. Projected on to a scale of eternal recurrence, this figures what for Shaw is the ultimate tragedy of Joan, that the heroic can never be accepted in its own time, by implication the earth will never be ready to receive its saints.

"Joan of Arc as the subject of a historical hypothesis, as Shaw would have it, an exponent of certain ways of thinking—there is something annoying about it. In her irreducible uniqueness she can be understood only by means of a sense of sympathetic admiration." We may well be inclined to agree here with the medieval historian Johan Huizinga. For all the extraordinary skill of Shaw's dialectic in identifying Joan with emergent Protestantism and nationalism, there *is* something annoying about it. It is hard to repress a feeling that this is no more than Shavian cleverness. And yet as Huizinga himself admits, what is remarkable is that Shaw did respond to Joan with the necessary "sense of sympathetic admiration," was inspired by "her irreducible uniqueness." There was in this an element of personal identification with Joan, as many critics were quick to point out. Joan's single-mindedness, her militant spirit, her directness in cutting through forms and ceremonies to the heart of the matter, all of these were essentially congenial to Shaw. He may well also have been attracted to her asceticism and her chaste asexuality. Earlier playwrights had romanticised Joan's relationship with her followers, particularly La Hire. Shaw instead lays great emphasis on her fellow soldiers who testified to her lack of sexual attractiveness. Joan at last gave Shaw a subject without what was for him the distracting nuisance of sex. Above all where he felt an affinity with Joan was in the capacity to be right when everyone else was wrong. There is a splendid anecdote told by Archibald Henderson—so well-turned that one suspects Shaw ghost-wrote it—about a lecture on Joan of Arc in which Shaw summed up all the various ways in which Joan "knew everybody's business better than they knew it themselves." He worked up to the deliberately provocative peroration: "After pondering over the matter for a time, I finally hit upon the perfect word which exactly describes Joan: *insufferable*." He got the reaction he was looking for from the lady who moved the vote of thanks, who pointed out "the one fundamental error into which Mr Shaw had fallen: it is not Joan of Arc, but Mr Bernard Shaw who is insufferable." From Shaw's point of view, they were both insufferable because they told the truths that nobody wanted to hear. Arland Ussher sees an element of nostalgia in this identification: "The hero who is laughed at, tolerated, petted, cannot conceal a certain envy for the heroine who is taken seriously and killed." Perhaps—Shaw, though courageous enough, was not the stuff of which martyrs are made. But he was convinced that he was, like Joan, if not a martyr at least a witness to an understanding of the world which could only come after him. Whether or not this now seems like a delusion, it was a real emotional source for *Saint Joan*.

To emphasise the element of personal identification might be to suggest, what some people have felt, that what we get is really a Joan cut down to Shavian size. Negatively it is true that there are aspects of Jeanne d'Arc that Shaw could not engage with imaginatively and which he omits from his representation. One of the most poignant features of the trial transcript is Jeanne's repeated pleas to be allowed to hear Mass, repeatedly refused except on the condition that she abandon her masculine dress. Although Shaw alludes to her devoutness in the preface, this very Catholic need to participate in the ritual of the Mass could not be made part of his "Protestant" Saint Joan. The certainty and resolution of Joan's faith were central for Shaw. As a result he could not really render the moving sense of humility expressed in the phrase Jeanne used so frequently in the trial: "I wait on Our Lord." Shaw's religion is a rational irrationalism without mystery and in making Joan a saint of creative evolution, he could scarcely present her with the attributes of a canonised saint of the Roman Catholic Church. Hence the ambiguity of the treatment of the voices and the miracles. But Shaw's imagination did go out to Joan, he did dramatise something of the extraordinary quality of her life. *Saint Joan* may not be tragedy; there is a deliberateness, a clarity about its form and significance which seem to take away the sense of awe and bewilderment which tragedy at its most profound evokes. It may not be Shaw's greatest play. But his capacity to write it commands a special respect and adds a dimension to his achievement as a playwright which it would otherwise have lacked.

Chronology

1856	Born on July 26, in Dublin, Ireland.
1876	Moves to London in the hopes of professional advancement and becomes a small-time journalist.
1879	Hired by the Edison Telephone Company and completes his first novel, *Immaturity*.
1880	Writes a second novel, *The Irrational Knot;* joins the Dialectical Society.
1881	Becomes a vegetarian in an attempt to cure migraine headaches and takes lessons in boxing; writes *Love Among the Artists*.
1882	Converts to socialism and completes his best novel, *Cashel Byron's Profession*.
1884	Falls among the Fabians; *An Unsocial Socialist* is serialized.
1885	Father dies.
1886–88	Works as an art critic and music critic for various journals.
1889	Publishes *Fabian Essays*.
1890	Begins work as a music critic for *The World;* lectures to the Fabian Society on Ibsen.
1891	Publishes *The Quintessence of Ibsenism*.
1892–93	*Widower's Houses, The Philanderer, Mrs Warren's Profession*.
1894	*Arms and the Man, Candida*.
1895	Starts as drama critic for the *Saturday Review. The Man of Destiny, You Never Can Tell*.
1896	*The Devil's Disciple*.

1898   Marries Charlotte Payne-Townshend. *Caesar and Cleopatra, The Perfect Wagnerite.*

1899   *Captain Brassbound's Conversion.*

1903   *Man and Superman.*

1904   *John Bull's Other Island.*

1905   Visits Ireland; *Major Barbara.*

1906   Meets Ellen Terry; *The Doctor's Dilemma, Our Theatres in the Nineties.*

1908   *Getting Married.*

1909   *Misalliance, The Shewing-up of Blanco Posnet.*

1911   *Fanny's First Play.*

1912   *Androcles and the Lion, Pygmalion;* friendship with Mrs. Patrick Campbell.

1914   *Common Sense about the War.*

1916–19   *Heartbreak House.*

1920   *Back to Methuselah.*

1923   *Saint Joan.*

1926   Receives the Nobel Prize for Literature—uses the prize money to support the publication of translations from Swedish literature.

1928   *The Intelligent Woman's Guide to Socialism, Capitalism, Sovietism, and Fascism.*

1929   *The Apple Cart.*

1931   *Ellen Terry and Bernard Shaw: A Correspondence.* Travels to U.S.S.R.

1932   *The Adventures of the Black Girl in Her Search for God.*

1933   Goes to America.

1934   *Collected Prefaces.*

1939   *In Good King Charles's Golden Days.*

1943   Wife dies.

1944   *Everybody's Political What's What.*

1950   Dies on November 13.

Contributors

HAROLD BLOOM, Sterling Professor of the Humanities at Yale University, is the author of *The Anxiety of Influence, Poetry and Repression,* and many other volumes of literary criticism. His forthcoming study, *Freud: Transference and Authority,* attempts a full-scale reading of all of Freud's major writings. A MacArthur Prize Fellow, he is general editor of five series of literary criticism published by Chelsea House. During 1987–88, he was appointed Charles Eliot Norton Professor of Poetry at Harvard University.

LOUIS L. MARTZ is Sterling Professor of English Emeritus at Yale University. His numerous books include *The Poetry of Meditation* and *The Paradise Within.*

LOUIS CROMPTON is Professor of English at the University of Nebraska. He is author of *Shaw the Dramatist* and writes extensively on homosexual literature and history. His most recent book is *Byron and Greek Love: Homophobia in 19th Century England.*

MARGERY M. MORGAN is Reader in English at the University of Lancaster. She is author of *A Drama of Political Man: A Study in the Plays of Harley Granville-Barker* and *The Shavian Playground.*

CHARLES A. BERST is Professor of English at the University of California at Los Angeles. He is author of *Bernard Shaw and the Art of Drama* and editor of *Shaw and Religion.*

WILLIAM SEARLE is Professor of English at the University of Pittsburgh.

NICHOLAS GRENE is Fellow and Director of Studies in Modern English at Trinity College, Dublin. In addition to a critical study of Shaw, he has written *Shakespeare, Jonson, Molière: The Comic Contract* and *Synge: A Critical Study of the Plays.*

Bibliography

Austin, Don. "Comedy through Tragedy: Dramatic Structure in *Saint Joan*." *Shaw Review* 8 (1965): 52–62.

Barnet, Sylvan. "Bernard Shaw on Tragedy." *PMLA* 71 (1956): 888–99.

Barr, Alan P. *Victorian Stage Pulpiteer: Bernard Shaw's Crusade*. Athens: University of Georgia Press, 1973.

Bentley, Eric. *Bernard Shaw*. Norfolk, Conn.: New Directions, 1946.

Boas, Frederick S. "Joan of Arc in Shakespeare, Schiller and Shaw." *Shakespeare Quarterly* 2 (1951) 34–45.

Brown, John Mason. "The Prophet and the Maid." *Saturday Review of Literature* 44 (1951): 27–29.

Chesterton, G. K. *George Bernard Shaw*. New York: Hill & Wang, 1956.

Cohen, M. A. "The 'Shavianization' of Cauchon." *Shaw Review* 20, no. 2 (1977): 63–70.

Dukore, Bernard F. *Bernard Shaw, Playwright: Aspects of Shavian Drama*. Columbia: University of Missouri Press, 1973.

Evans, T. F., ed. *Shaw: The Critical Heritage*. London: Routledge & Kegan Paul, 1976.

Fielden, John. "Shaw's *Saint Joan* as Tragedy." *Twentieth-Century Literature* 3 (1957): 59–67.

Fraser, G. S. *The Modern Writer and His World: Continuity and Innovation in Twentieth-Century Literature*. New York: Praeger, 1953.

Gassner, John. *Ideas in Drama*. New York: Columbia University Press, 1964.

Gibbs, A. M. *The Art and Mind of Shaw*. London: Macmillan, 1983.

Harris, Frank. *Bernard Shaw*. Garden City, N.Y.: Garden City Publishing, 1931.

Henderson, Archibald. *Table-Talk of G. B. S.* London: Chapman & Hall, 1925.

———. *Bernard Shaw, Playboy and Prophet*. New York: D. Appleton, 1932.

———. *George Bernard Shaw: Man of the Century*. New York: Appleton-Century-Crofts, 1956.

Irvine, William. *The Universe of G. B. S.* New York: Whittlesey House, 1949.

Kaul, A. N. "George Bernard Shaw: From Anti-Romance to Pure Fantasy." In *The Action of English Comedy: Studies in the Encounter of Abstraction and Experience from Shakespeare to Shaw*. New Haven: Yale University Press, 1970.

Kronenberger, Louis, ed. *George Bernard Shaw: A Critical Survey*. Cleveland: World Publishing, 1953.

Langner, Lawrence. *G. B. S. and the Lunatic.* New York: Atheneum, 1963.

MacCarthy, Desmond. *Shaw.* London: MacGibbon & Kee, 1951.

Macksoud, S. John, and Ross Altman. "Voices in Opposition: A Burkeian Rhetoric of *Saint Joan.*" *The Quarterly Journal of Speech* 57 (1971): 140–46.

Meisel, Martin. *Shaw and the Nineteenth-Century Theater.* Princeton, N.J.: Princeton University Press, 1963.

Mills, John A. *Language and Laughter: Comic Diction in the Plays of Bernard Shaw.* Tucson: University of Arizona Press, 1969.

Murray, T. Douglas, ed. *Jeanne D'Arc, Maid of Orleans, Deliverer of France; Being the Story of her Life, her Achievements, and her Death, as attested on Oath and Set forth in the Original Documents.* New York: McClure, Phillips, 1902.

Nethercot, Arthur H. *Men and Supermen: The Shavian Portrait Gallery.* New York: B. Blom, 1966.

O'Donovan, John. *G. B. Shaw.* Dublin: Gill & Macmillan, 1983.

Ohmann, Richard M. *Shaw: The Style and the Man.* Middletown, Conn.: Wesleyan University Press, 1962.

Robertson, J. M. *Mr. Shaw and "The Maid."* London: Richard Cobden-Sanderson, 1925.

Roy, R. N. *George Bernard Shaw's Historical Plays.* Delhi: Macmillan, 1976.

Schoeps, Karl Heinz. "Epic Structures in the Plays of Bernard Shaw and Bertolt Brecht." In *Essays on Brecht: Theatre and Politics,* edited by Siegfried Mews and Herbert Knust. Chapel Hill: University of North Carolina Press, 1974.

Smith, Warren S., ed. *Bernard Shaw's Plays.* New York: Norton, 1970.

Solomon, Stanley. "*Saint Joan* as Epic Tragedy." *Modern Drama* (February 1964): 437–49.

Stewart, J. I. M. *Eight Modern Writers.* Oxford: Oxford University Press, 1963.

Stoppel, Hans. "Shaw and Sainthood." *English Studies* 36 (1955): 49–63.

Turco, Alfred Jr. *Shaw's Moral Vision: The Self and Salvation.* Ithaca: Cornell University Press, 1976.

Tyson, Brian. *The Story of Shaw's* Saint Joan. Kingston: McGill-Queen's University Press, 1982.

Valency, Maurice. *The Cart and the Trumpet: The Plays of George Bernard Shaw.* New York: Oxford University Press, 1973.

Weintraub, Stanley. *The Unexpected Shaw: Biographical Approaches to G. B. S. and His Work.* New York: Ungar, 1982.

———. Saint Joan *Fifty Years After: 1923/24–1973/74.* Baton Rouge: Louisiana State University Press, 1973.

Whitman, Robert. *Shaw and the Play of Ideas.* Ithaca: Cornell University Press, 1977.

Williams, Raymond. *Drama from Ibsen to Brecht.* New York: Oxford University Press, 1968.

Wisenthal, J. L. *The Marriage of Contraries: Bernard Shaw's Middle Plays.* Cambridge: Harvard University Press, 1974.

Acknowledgments

"The Saint as Tragic Hero: *Saint Joan* and *Murder in the Cathedral*" by Louis L. Martz from *Tragic Themes in Western Literature,* edited by Cleanth Brooks, © 1955 by Yale University Press. Reprinted by permission of Yale University Press.

"A Hagiography of Creative Evolution" (originally entitled *"Saint Joan"*) by Louis Crompton from *Shaw the Dramatist* by Louis Crompton, © 1969 by the University of Nebraska Press. Reprinted by permission of the University of Nebraska Press.

"The Histories" by Margery M. Morgan from *The Shavian Playground: An Exploration of the Art of George Bernard Shaw* by Margery M. Morgan, © 1972 by Margery M. Morgan. Reprinted by permission of Methuen & Co., Ltd.

"Saint Joan: Spiritual Epic as Tragicomedy" by Charles A. Berst from *Bernard Shaw and the Art of Drama* by Charles A. Berst, © 1973 by the Board of Trustees of the University of Illinois. Reprinted by permission of the University of Illinois Press.

"The Saint and the Skeptic: Joan of Arc and George Bernard Shaw" (originally entitled "Shaw and Vitalism" and "Joan as Galtonic Visualizer") by William Searle from *The Saint and the Skeptics: Joan of Arc in the Work of Mark Twain, Anatole France, and Bernard Shaw* by William Searle, © 1976 by Wayne State University Press. Reprinted by permission.

"Shavian History" by Nicholas Grene from *Bernard Shaw: A Critical View* by Nicholas Grene, © 1984 by Nicholas Grene. Reprinted by permission of St. Martin's Press and Macmillan Press Ltd., London and Basingstoke.

Index